D1457474

ENGLISH AND THE NATIONAL CURRICULUM

Bedford Way Series
Published by Kogan Page in association with the Institute of
Education, University of London

THE BEDFORD WAY SERIES

ENGLISH AND THE NATIONAL CURRICULUM: COX'S REVOLUTION?

Edited by
KEN JONES

Contributors:
Ken Jones, Anne Turvey,
Chris Richards, Robert Owens

**KOGAN
PAGE**

Published in association with
The Institute of Education, University of London

First published in 1992

Apart from any fair dealing for the purposes of research or private
study, or criticism of review, as permitted under the Copyright, Designs
and Patents Act, 1988, this publication may only be reproduced, stored
or transmitted, in any form or by any means, with the prior permission
in writing of the publishers, or in the case of reprographic reproduction
in accordance with the terms of licences issued by the Copyright Licens-
ing Agency. Enquiries concerning reproduction outside those terms
should be sent to the publishers at the undermentioned address:

Kogan Page Limited
120 Pentonville Road
London N1 9JN

© Institute of Education, 1992

British Library Cataloguing in Publication Data

A CIP record for this book is available from the British Library.

ISBN 0 7494 0641 0

Typeset by Witwell Ltd, Southport
Printed and bound in Great Britain by
Biddles Ltd, Guildford

Contents

Notes on Contributors

Ken Jones, **Anne Turvey** and **Chris Richards** began teaching in London in the 1970s. Since 1989 they have worked in the Department of English, Media and Drama at the Institute of Education, University of London.

Robert Owens has taught English at Newham Community College, East London, since 1990.

Chapter One
The 'Cox Report': Working for Hegemony

Ken Jones

Culture and politics

'There is an urgent need', wrote Professor C. B. Cox in 1981, 'for new Conservative initiatives in education'.[1] History has been kind to Brian Cox: since the mid-1980s 'new Conservative initiatives' have accumulated to the point where the landscape of education in England and Wales has been substantially remade. The chapters in this book focus upon one of the smaller features of that remaking – the model of English in the National Curriculum constructed by Professor Cox himself, visionary turned planner and chair of the Subject Working Group on English which reported in June 1989.[2] It is with the detail of the Report's arguments and recommendations that we attempt to engage.

We engage with them from a particular direction. Cox would be the first to recognise that understanding his Report (henceforward 'Cox') requires the establishment of a wider context. His own writings[3] make clear that 'culture' is a central term of reference for the Report; the relationship between unity and plurality, national culture and diverse subcultures is among its main preoccupations. Our argumentative rendezvous with 'Cox' is made, more often than not, on this cultural ground: we approach debates about the nature of English through disputes about culture. Indeed, we do not think the Report becomes comprehensible until it is viewed in this way. The chapters by Robert Owens, Chris Richards and Anne Turvey thus attempt to make cultural sense of 'Cox'. In doing so, they address instead some questions which have been by-passed by the National Curriculum but which remain central to thinking about students, schools, teaching and learning.

An early consultative document from the DES expressed a truth

about the National Curriculum with a clarity that no later presentation has matched. 'All pupils', it stated, 'regardless of sex, ethnic
origin and geographical location [should] have access to broadly the
same good and relevant curriculum and programmes of study'. In
this parade of 'equal opportunity' keywords, 'relevant', 'regardless
of', 'access', 'sex', 'ethnic origin' pass before the reader with
anaesthetising familiarity, until the incongruity of two of the terms
provokes a sudden awakening. How can 'regardless of' and 'relevant'
be bracketed together? Surely 'broadly the same curriculum' cannot
be 'relevant' to 'all pupils', 'regardless of sex, ethnic origin and
geographical location'?[4] The later chapters in this book begin, in a
sense, with these questions. In exploring the relationship between
the cultures of students and the cultures of schools, they replace
'regardless of' with 'having regard to'. They suggest that learning is
always a social process, which develops in and through the
encounters between the experience and the discourses of students
and the institutional and intellectual practices of the school. The
authors reflect on what their own experience as teachers of English
and Media Studies has taught them about learning, in the context of
such relationships. In doing so, they point to forms of curricular and
pedagogic practice which, being based on a kind of dialogue with
students, have little in common with the extraordinarily prescriptive
'relevance' of the DES. Out of this experience comes a critical
response to 'Cox', which takes shape at the point where issues of
culture and issues of learning meet. It is a response which concerns
itself not so much with statements of attainment and programmes of
study, as with the general orientation to the subject which 'Cox'
seeks to effect. We are interested in what 'Cox' says about the
cultures of students and the culture of the nation, and about the way
in which these different spheres of existence are to be related
through the learning of English.

'Culture', then, is one focus for our – critical – engagement with
the National Curriculum. The second focus, with which this present
chapter is particularly concerned, is on its politics. In the politics of
reform, 'equal opportunity' was for a long time the key organising
term. A term open to many interpretations, it linked in its most
common usage the promise of wider access to a worthwhile
education with the expectation that raising general levels of
achievement would make the economy more efficient and com-
petitive. It contributed to the development of a school system
tending towards – if certainly not achieving – uniformity of

provision. Things have changed. Conservative education policy rests on different principles: the strong elements of 'choice' embedded in 'opting out' and 'open enrolment', and the promotion of inter-school competition and cost-cutting through 'local management of schools' suggest a system in which differentiated and unequal provision will be the norm.

This system can be criticised on grounds of social justice. It can also be looked at in another light: Conservative reform, it is argued by many critics,[5] will not substantially improve the relative performance of education in England and Wales. Anguished comparisons with European success will continue. What cautious, partial and under-funded policies of equal opportunity were unable to achieve, full-blooded marketisation will not better. The redevelopment of differentiated schooling will not increase general levels of education to the point where England emulates Germany or France. Thus most of the policies associated with themes of choice and market have been attacked by those who wish to see education taking a central part in a project of technical and economic regeneration.

The National Curriculum is the great exception to this sceptical view of the effects of Conservative change. It is now, – states the *Schools Charter* produced by *The Independent* – 'thankfully, a consensual feature of British life.'[6] From 1988 to mid-1991, this was certainly true.[7] Born in political controversy, the National Curriculum has swiftly become part of the common sense of educational policy. Many of those who spoke 10 years ago of radical change are among its present supporters.[8] It is worth considering how this turnaround has happened. Explanations related to 'betrayal' or 'career interests' are not helpful. Nor, in any complete sense – are those that relate to the tactical dimensions of the issue. Of course, some people, recognising an unfavourable balance of forces when they see one, have chosen to modify the system from within. Others, who had feared that the triumphal mood of late-1980s Conservatism would bring something far worse, have been relieved to settle for the compromises engineered by the Subject Working Groups. But to concentrate on these responses misses a deeper level of adherence to the National Curriculum project, and to the arguments about the failings of state education on which the case for it has been made to rest. Invested in this Conservative initiative are many non-Conservative hopes that it will realise the objectives of 'equal opportunity' reform. Modernisa-

tion, standardisation, and the establishment of normative expectations for all students will improve the education of those whom a
system based on local control and teacher-led innovation has so far
failed.

   This assessment of the National Curriculum – as a means of
continuing equal opportunity reform – is lent a sort of back-handed
plausibility by the response of the Conservative right, which has
condemned with increasing sharpness the products of the Subject
Working Groups and sought with growing success to limit their
effects. Even Kenneth Baker, who, as Education Secretary, com-
missioned the Cox Report, 'very much disliked it'.[9] By contrast,
according to Brian Cox, those who have to implement the National
Curriculum have greeted his report with enthusiasm.[10] In the face of
these complexities, this chapter seeks to explain the paradoxes of
the report's reception and thus shed light on the more general
politics of the National Curriculum. But the chapter aims not only
to explain but to criticise. Though it recognises in the National
Curriculum aspects of a modernising project, it does not, overall,
evaluate it in positive terms: in addition to registering the impact of
the National Curriculum, the chapter also seeks to set out the terms
in which it can be criticised. The conceptual framework with which
it tries to work needs thus to sustain both an understanding and a
critique. Where to begin?

Passive revolution

In some of the more laconic pages of the *Prison Notebooks*
Antonio Gramsci reflected on the triumph of the fascism which had
imprisoned him.[11] He borrowed from the work of a conservative
thinker of the Risorgimento a term which he used to conceptualise
the process of change that fascism was bringing about: 'passive
revolution'. My chapter, trying to explain and to criticise the
National Curriculum, borrows the term from Gramsci. The contexts, of course, are different. He was meditating on the failure of
socialist revolution; I am considering the present difficulties of
educational reform. To place the two experiences side-by-side is to
risk not just the imperfections of analogy but also the most bathetic
of contrasts. Schools are not factories; Conservatism is not fascism,
and progressive reform is not social transformation. Gramsci's
categories have to be reworked, and there is a danger of looseness in
any such act of translation. Even so, the attempt is, I think, more
illuminating than it is troubling. Gramsci's use of analogy, compari-

son and metaphor as interpretive devices was often productive; and placing the National Curriculum alongside Gramsci's summary of fascist achievements sparks the same sense of surprised recognition as some of Gramsci's own metaphors and juxtapositions.

The Italian left had interpreted the events of the years after World War I as a sign that capitalism in Italy was incapable of further development. Gramsci observed, by contrast, that Mussolini's government, however authoritarian, had brought about important changes in the economy – diminishing its chronic problems, developing it along more rational lines, and coordinating state policy with that of private industry. This was not a reason for Gramsci to lessen his opposition to fascism; but it was a social fact, with whose effects the left needed to come to terms. He analysed the new situation in this way:

> The ideological hypothesis could be presented in the following terms: that there is a passive revolution involved in the fact that – through the legislative intervention of the state . . . relatively far-reaching modifications are being introduced into the country's economic structure in order to accentuate the 'plan of production' element; in other words that socialisation and co-operation in the sphere of production are being increased, without, however touching . . . individual and group appropriation of profit . . . . Whether or not such a schema could be put into practice, and to what extent, is only of relative importance. What is important from the political and ideological point of view is that it is capable of creating – and indeed does create – a period of expectation and hope, especially in certain Italian social groups such as the great mass of urban and rural petit bourgeois. It thus reinforces the hegemonic system and the forces of military and civil coercion at the disposal of the traditional ruling classes.'[12]

The passage describes a process of 'passive revolution'. Elsewhere in Gramsci's notes, the term is used interchangeably with 'revolution/ restoration'. This latter formulation has the particular value of drawing attention to the two-sidedness of the changes Gramsci is analysing, changes that are both responses to real problems of national development *and* attempts to reinforce the hegemony and authoritarian rule of the dominant class. For 'passive revolution' ('revolution/restoration') involves an effort *from the right* to respond to historic problems of development through, in this case, a greater level of planning and state intervention. In some respects,

it organises great and not irrational change, as the state introduces
elements of compulsion into its relationship with Italian industry.
But this rationality intertwines with, and is diminished by, the
second feature of 'passive revolution'. 'Individual and group appropriation of profit' are not touched: fundamental social relations
have not altered. Passive revolution is a means of ensuring that
these relations are perpetuated, not by achieving stasis, but by
renewing hegemony – by changing the *means* by which a class
organises leadership so that they are appropriate to new conditions.
'Things must change,' wrote Lampedusa, 'so that they can remain
the same.' Gramsci would have admired *The Leopard*, a novel *par
excellence* of passive revolution. He would have appreciated particularly, I think, Lampedusa's account of the ball at Palazzo
Ponteleone, where the aristocracy and the once-rebellious parvenus
of Palermo fete the general who has crushed the last rising of
radical nationalism and left the fruits of the Risorgimento to be
savoured by this alliance of old wealth and new.[13] Passive revolution, Lampedusa understood, is a complex process; it involves the
pre-empting of revolutionary change, the co-opting of some new
energies and the repression of others. Gramsci, writing of the 'raised
expectations' of some social groups, and the coercion of others,
shares his understanding. Passive revolution is not simply the
establishment of new economic or political or educational
structures; it is a process which by involving people directly –
though in a subordinate role – in the creation of these structures
draws them into new forms of hegemony.

Passive revolution does not involve the mass of the population in
planning the process of transformation it aims to bring about.
Indeed, in the case of fascism it developed precisely on the basis of
the severe defeat of working-class and peasant insurrection. But, as
other elaborators of Gramsci's work have suggested, it has had
nevertheless an important impact on mass socialist organisations.[14]
Passive revolution addresses historic issues of development that the
left had thought were its own property. Communists and socialists
had claimed that only their programme could introduce the elements of planning that the further development of the productive
forces required. By answering these claims with a practical programme of its own, fascism was able to appropriate some of the
themes of the left's discourse of social transformation. In doing so it
was able for a period to disorientate and throw into crisis the left's
alternative project, all the more effectively, of course, because of the

defeat and repression of left organisations. In this situation, and in similar situations since, supporters of alternative projects have found themselves in practice (if not in theory) accepting this powerlessness, to the point where they become politically integrated into the new system.[15] Reform then becomes much less a transitional stage to socialism than an inoculation against more substantial change. 'Restoration' may contain a 'revolutionary' element, but it is restoration all the same.

Lastly, there is the further 'doubleness' of passive revolution. Not only is it a combination of revolution and restoration, but of the 'imaginary' and the 'real'. Gramsci's description moves ambiguously between what *is* (far-reaching modifications in the economy) and what *might be* (a 'schema' which may or may not be put into practice). Passive revolution, he suggests, is a process that may be lived most vividly in the imagination. Promise, expectation and the rhetorical resolution of real problems and conflicts are as important to its effects as the strengthening of the economy or a change in the constitution.

In all these respects, 'passive revolution' has an application beyond the historical contexts to which Gramsci applies it. It suggests a means of understanding the double-sidedness of some kinds of change. At the same time, it offers an explanation of their attractiveness to particular social groups and of their value to a project of hegemony. Such double-sidedness is absent from most understandings of the National Curriculum. On the militant left, there have been denunciations of its centralising and essentially Conservative nature.[16] Elsewhere, amid the mainstream of reform, there has been approval of its contribution to modernisation and to equal opportunity. The first kind of response cannot explain the National Curriculum's popular appeal. The second subordinates its own historic principles to a project whose commitment to progressive educational objectives does not, finally, survive interrogation. What this chapter seeks to capture is the inter-relationship between 'revolution' and 'restoration' within the National Curriculum project.[17] In doing so, it will also seek to explain the processes of hegemony that are at work in the National Curriculum: the ways in which 'revolution' and 'restoration' are intertwined in a project that both addresses the concerns of reformers and binds them, at least temporarily, within forms of consent to dominant ideologies.

Passive revolution involves addressing the 'unsolved problems' of society. So, in a very strong sense, does the National Curriculum. It has qualities that allow a special status to be claimed for it, as a vigorous and critical heir to the incomplete reforms of the 1960s and 1970s. The comprehensive school lacked a comprehensive, remodelled curriculum. One way of understanding the reports of the Subject Working Groups is to see them as an attempt to provide this unified curriculum for a mass education. It is possible, of course, to point to the inconsistencies surrounding the National Curriculum: public schools are exempt from it, and there is continual Conservative pressure to introduce elements of 'twin-tracking' at 14 which would diminish the project's claims to offer a universal entitlement.[18] Nevertheless, the main lines of support remain clear, and are set out very lucidly in Bob Moon's *A Guide to the National Curriculum*:

> Advocates of a National Curriculum can be found right across the political spectrum. . . . For many educationists the logic that under-pins the provision of free and compulsory schooling also extends to what is taught. . . . A National Curriculum provides a framework that, in theory, rules out such inconsistencies and inequalities in provision. Pupils and their parents now have access to public documents that describe the subjects and content to be covered at each stage of development. . . . In the past, the expectations of what many children could achieve have been unnecessarily low. A defined framework, with attainment targets, could lead to higher expec-tations and improved standards.[19]

Moon's account links together a set of themes relating to entitle-ment, equality and accountability with an educational programme relying on standardisation and normative expectation. The whole ensemble of justifications recalls very forcibly one of the central points of 'passive revolution': it involves a promise to complete the *unfinished business* of earlier periods by clearing away the obstacles which then impeded change. In this case, the central state is intervening to accomplish the curriculum upheaval which older educational arrangements – teacher autonomy, local control – could not succeed in organising. Its intervention greatly increases the degree of direction, planning and monitoring involved in the organisation of learning. By doing so, it can claim to have cut through the knot of problems which reforming traditions were not able to unravel. Thus it can present itself to parents as an empowering agency, and to industry as a dynamic moderniser. To teachers, not yet recovered from the batterings of the 1980s, it can claim to bring an authoritative clarity to their work, based not on the imposition of a Conservative programme, but on a distillation of their own best practice. If 'passive revolution' is a combination of 'revolution' and 'restoration' then these developments belong very much on the side of 'revolution'.

The 'restorationist' aspect of the National Curriculum, however, can barely be glimpsed in Moon's account. From other perspectives it is more visible. Kenneth Clark's decision[20] to sever 'history' from 'current affairs', for instance, was a reminder that 'restoration' need not be subtle in its operations.[21] But restorationist effects are usually achieved more through the inner logic of the National Curriculum system and the Education Reform Act than through external intervention of the Clark variety. Hegemony, as Terry Eagleton reminds us, is after all a matter of 'lived, habitual social practice' and not only of the power of 'systems of ideas'[22] It is from this point of view that we should understand some of the effects of government-promoted change. They have shifted the focus of curriculum initiative away from the classroom. While teachers have yet to recover from the defeat of militant unionism, or to set limits to the increased workload that they have faced since the later 1980s, school managements have been enabled to take the lead in defining objectives and in setting a context for the work of individual teachers or departments. Since innovation in, say, secondary school English was in the past closely related to teacher autonomy, this change in school culture has had important effects. For their full impact on the commitments and priorities of teachers to be understood, the curriculum and assessment procedures of the new system have to be grasped in this context – to which they add a new level of prescriptiveness. In keeping with the passivity of this process of great change, teachers become the deliverers of systems whose general purposes they have had no role in developing. Their ability to resist such change, moreover, has been reduced by the legal definition of teachers' responsibilities set out in the Teachers' Pay and Conditions Act of 1987, a measure which has taught teachers the meaning of coercion.

Coercion, the absence of effective popular involvement and the blocking of potential alternative projects are features marked on the harsh face of passive revolution. Yet, as Gramsci noted, it has a more seductive side. Part of the National Curriculum's attractiveness is the bracing promise it makes of what Cox calls 'revolution-

ary changes'.[23] It will rid schools of archaic pedagogic practices –
the teacher-dominated classroom, for instance – and will force
teachers to reconsider, in the light of modern thinking, the essen-
tials of their subjects. At the same time, it cushions the shock of the
new by suggesting that, in most respects, it is no more than a
continuation of the best of the old – renegotiated, but not
abandoned. Curricular changes, as we shall see, are thus presented
as *continuations*, elaborations of old reforming themes. They are
also said to be *reconciliations* of unresolved, sometimes bitter
arguments about the nature of a particular subject. Out of the
opposing poles of 'progress' and 'tradition', National Curriculum
apologists claim to have arrived at a higher-level synthesis.It is at
these moments – Cox's treatment of grammar is an example – when
conflicts are soothed and new pledges made, that an attention to
discursive strategies can be especially valuable. It may be that by
disturbing the reassurances of documents like 'Cox' the underlying
processes of revolution/restoration can be revealed.

Cox – a life in politics

A pamphlet issued by the National Association for the Teaching of
English in 1989 welcomed 'the philosophy of English which underpins the [Cox] report'. 'The principles of a sound English
curriculum' had 'by and large, been recognised' and the Report was
'a distillation of current thinking and practice that is principled,
coherent, realistic and imaginative.'[24] Judgements like these mis-
recognise 'Cox'. It is interesting, however, that they can be made at
all. The Report is the culmination of an intellectually consistent
career, spent largely on the right of educational politics. Yet it is
welcomed, without insincerity, in the publication of a body long
associated with progressive traditions. What has the Report done to
gain itself such a reception?

The crucial point is that 'Cox' rejects the definitions of English
offered by the radical right, and endorsed at one time by the
Secretary of State and by the (then) Prime Minister. Traditional
models of grammar are criticised; the canon has lost its centrality;
'basic skills' are a concept with no currency in the report. Instead, it
validates some themes that have been closely associated with
progressive traditions in English teaching: the importance of talking and listening; the centring of classroom reading on 'response'
rather than 'comprehension'. As well as holding on to these features
of progressive pedagogy, 'Cox' maintains links with other aspects of

the reforming tradition. It is notable among Subject Working Groups for its attention to 'equal opportunities' and to the needs of 'bilingual' learners. It has produced an account of Standard English acclaimed for its democratic recognition of the value of non-standard dialects.[25] It legitimises and (according to one of those who drafted it) embodies a commitment to cultural analysis and to critical thinking.[26] In these latter two respects, its supporters claim it is superior to progressive traditions of English teaching. In place of what Cox has called the 'muddled vitalism'[27] of the 1960s, it offers – particularly in its programmes of language study – an intellectual rigour. It aims at a *disciplined* creativity.

'Cox', then, has been able to absorb selectively and to transcend the 'radical' past. This is an achievement that allows us to place it firmly within the frame of 'revolution'. In a practical sense, many educationists have come to the same positive conclusion, most with some surprise. The life's work of Professor Cox had suggested a much greater hostility towards the norms of English teaching than the report actually expressed. Yet, although noted, the paradoxes of the relationship between Cox and 'Cox' have been little explored. It is valuable, I think, to do so, not because it is possible to trace the hand of a single maker in the composition of an official document, but because a presentation of aspects of Professor Cox's life's work allow the Report to be read in a light which shows up some unobserved features. In this light it is possible to see, beneath the reconciliation of 'progress' with 'tradition', the outlines of an approach to cultural relationships which reveals the distinctive traces of a conservative mode of thought: the acceptance of socio-linguistics and of 'equal opportunities' is conditional upon a marked deradicalisation in their emphases and a limitation of their scope.

Since the 1950s, Cox has been an activist intellectual – an organiser. He has been adept at developing publications and networks that have enabled the popularisation of a fairly consistent body of ideas. At the core has been a concern with developing a 'common culture'. In particular conjunctures, this concern has inclined Cox to the political left, to support for the Labour Party. At others, it has led him towards a conservative politics. Over the last 25 years it is the latter trend which has prevailed: 'common culture' has not served Cox as an inclusive category, embracing the range of popular experience. It has instead been tied to the values of a particular literary tradition.

In 1959, with A. E. Dyson, Cox founded *Critical Quarterly*, a magazine whose 'aim was to ensure that high standards of lucid English and a wide appreciation of great literature remained powerful elements of our common culture'. By the mid-1960s, the magazine was selling more than 5000 copies of each issue. 'Teachers of English from about half the grammar schools in Britain were among its subscribers'.[28] Despite the threat the party posed to grammar school education, Cox was a Labour voter in the General Election of 1966.[29] Soon afterwards though, repelled by Labour's educational politics and appalled at the 'student misbehaviour' of the late 1960s,[30] he co-edited the first of a series of critical pamphlets, the *Black Papers*. Again, his initiative was successful. The first two *Black Papers* sold 80,000 copies.[31] In them, Cox published criticisms of Labour's commitment to comprehensive schools, of its lurch towards progressive educational philosophy and of the delinquency and student militancy which were among the main effects of its 'utopian idealism'. These tendencies he saw as betrayals of the 'grammar school concepts of discipline and hard work',[32] which maintained 'the highest standards' and 'the finest academic and cultural values'.[33] Labour, he argued (from the viewpoint of 'equal opportunity' in its weakest form) was betraying the interests of the 'bright' working-class child, who was cut off by progressive relativism and licence from the standards and the culture which were not only valuable ends in themselves, but also the prime means of individual empowerment.

Cox considered that the campaigns of the *Black Papers* were 'more educational than political'.[34] Nevertheless, by 1972 he had joined the Conservative Party, in whose think-tanks he was soon immersed.[35] In the 1970s he contributed to the further undermining of 'progressive' dominance. As well as editing the *Black Papers*, he chaired the National Council for Educational Standards (NCES), a body which pioneered the rethinking of Conservative education policy that took place in the 1980s.. The intellectual standpoint from which he worked remained constant, and is summed up in the description given by one sympathetic commentator of his evidence to the Bullock Committee in 1975:

> the pursuance by some teachers of a value-free concept of culture (a popular culture) had . . . been one cause of the dilution of English teaching and the reaction against spelling and grammar . . . [he] had informed the Bullock Committee that an explicit grammar was an

acceptance of order and that the 'new revolutionaries' deliberately rejected such structuring of experience.

Cox, writes his interpreter, in this way symbolised the 'preservationist' view: that the 'structuring of experience provided by the traditional style of schooling was essential, both to the preservation of individual humanity and the nation's common culture'.[36]
Preservationist he may have been, but by the mid-1970s Cox had realised that the grammar school environment in which appreciation of great literature had thrived could not easily be restored.[37] The fight for standards and for a particular version of a 'common culture' had to be carried into the comprehensive school. In 1981, in a pamphlet written for the Conservative Political Centre, he joined battle with the left in a 'cultural war over values'.[38] 'Each small detail', he wrote then, ' – the attack on exams, the abandonment of form positions, of prizes and speech day – is part of the new consciousness, the new hegemony'.[39] This hegemony was indifferent towards 'academic excellence' which depended not on 'impractical utopian schemes' such as tertiary colleges, but on the nurturing of a 'community of scholars'. 'In our traditional sixth forms', Cox believed, 'in independent, grammar and good comprehensive schools, an environment is created where high standards . . . are accepted as normal'.[40] The pamphlet thus equated excellence with selection, low standards with egalitarianism. While tolerating the good comprehensive school, it defended the values and the practices of traditional academic life. It conveyed no sense of dialogue with subordinate or emergent cultures. This latter point, it will be argued, is the core of 'Coxism' and has survived intact the changes his work has undergone since 1981.
In 1985, the NCES organised a conference entitled 'The Search for Common Ground'. By this time, the polemics of the right had softened. Cox, writing in 1984, believed that the *Black Papers* had managed to 'curb the excesses of progressive education'.[41] The NCES, likewise, thought it had been successful in making 'the dangers of lowered standards' a central issue in educational politics.[42] Now it was time to draw 'educationalists and politicians' into the work of turning general consensus into concrete policy. In this less embattled context, Cox spoke to the conference about 'The Arts', and turned his attention to a new threat.[43] His criticisms of government education policy were sharp. It was not well-disposed to the arts and creativity. It was under-funding university educa-

tion. It was supporting a 'new vocationalism' which would 'harm
the quality of life throughout the community'. 'High standards in
English' were foremost among the requirements for 'an educated
community in a democratic society', but the 'shift of resources from
Arts to Sciences' was placing such standards under threat. Nothing
Cox said indicated a shift in his basic positions on 'culture' and
'quality'; but the terms had now become a standpoint from which to
criticise the 'utilitarianism' of the government.

In championing 'culture' and 'creativity' against vocationalism,
Cox was also, of course, enabling a possible link-up in defence of
'creativity' with those 'progressive' teachers he had spent two
decades attacking. In the composition, four years later, of the
Report, this possibility was realised. 'Cox' joins with 'progressive'
teachers in criticising the grammatical fetishism of the right, and
rejects the idea that English should have a vocational bias. But this
pact against the right also serves a hegemonic purpose in the
report's dealings with the left. The ideas of 'culture' and 'standards'
to which Cox had devoted 20 years are not sacrificed; but many
conceptions associated with progressive reform undergo substantial
change, even at points where they seem to have received legitimation.

Cox's repositioning of himself in relation to central issues
continued after 1985. In a lengthy commentary on the Report, Cox
refers to the historic conflicts within English teaching which his
committee has been able to overcome. In the 1950s and 1960s, he
asserts, 'some senior educationalists committed themselves to
fashionable ideas about teaching English: that children would learn
to read naturally . . . or that their writing should be the product not
of craft but of free expression'. Fortunately, 'by the late 1980s such
excesses had been banished from the best classrooms'. 'The teachers
in my Group', writes Cox, 'all acknowledged the need for a sensible
balance between the formal and the informal'.[44]

Viewed in this way, the central conflicts of the last 20 years have
been fought along the axis of formality and informality. Revisiting
the battlefield, Cox reinterprets what happened there. It was not so
much a 'cultural war over values' as a series of skirmishes against
'excess'. This is an intellectual, bowdlerising manoeuvre of some
importance. Whereas the *Black Papers* wrote of a crisis which was
cultural as well as methodological, the Cox of the 1990s, not
wishing to reopen controversies that he feels have been resolved in
his favour, limits the area of dispute in ways which render it

politically less controversial. At the same time he takes care to
signal his distance from the traditional right by drawing attention
to his creative credentials. 'For over ten years,' he insists, 'I had
been conducting a campaign to make creative writing a central
feature of the English curriculum'.[45] Had Kenneth Baker known of
this, Cox implies, he would have been much less keen to involve
him in planning the National Curriculum.

The effect of moves like these is to obscure the ways in which
'Cox' intervenes in debates about English teaching and culture.
They help create that impression of compromise, continuity and
consensus that is essential to the Report's soft landing. But
compromise, of course, is at least a two-sided process; and the
success of 'Cox' depends as much on the willingness of 'progressive'
English teachers to recognise themselves in the report as it does on
the substantial shift in position of the report's chief organiser. One
of the reasons 'Cox' could accomplish the manoeuvre was a lack of
self-awareness within progressive English teaching. In practice, the
range of what counted as progressive teaching was very wide. It
stretched from the espousal of particular teaching *techniques*[46] to
the attempt to work out radical political and cultural positions in
terms of classroom relationships and practice. But this very diverse
activity was not accompanied by parallel efforts to clarify and
debate differences. Some, undoubtedly, tried to make central in the
'English curriculum the kinds of knowledge and experience which
would give working-class pupils an understanding of inequality and
its causes'.[47] In doing so, they raised important questions –
implicitly critical of aspects of progressivism – about the content of
the curriculum, and the problematic relationship between the
culture of school and the cultures of school-students. They remained a minority, however, and were not able to stimulate a lasting
debate about purpose. Thus, although a penumbra of social
criticism surrounded the intentions of many English teachers, for
most of them 'progressive education' was articulated as a matter of
method. To say this is not to deny the importance of the issues they
foregrounded: the centrality of talk to learning, the insistence on
the active role of the learner are 'methodological' principles far
from narrow in their scope. It is, though, to suggest that an
emphasis on the *activity* of the learner does not necessarily involve
recognising and articulating the issues of social and cultural conflict
that are raised in the encounter between real, 'historical' learners
and the practices of formal education. It is the prevalence of the

'weaker' forms of self-definition, often lagging behind the actual practice of English teachers, that allows Cox to claim so confidently that his Report synthesises once-opposed traditions of English. If the more radical currents within the progressive movement had been able to articulate the purposes of their work with greater clarity and if, in doing so, they had been able to make clear what distinguished their practice from other forms of progressivism, then it is unlikely that 'Cox's' claim to have melded all that was valuable in different 'schools' of English teaching could have been made to such great effect.

The argument of this chapter is not that 'Cox' builds its curriculum on pure *Black Paper* foundations. The comments of NATE are to a considerable extent accurate: the report *does* validate many aspects of current 'good practice' in English teaching. At the same time, however, it maintains a resolute blankness towards the cultures of school-students and of the communities in which they live. In this respect it has brought about a revision of important aspects of English teaching, a revision whose nature can be highlighted by drawing attention to the continuity of Cox's present positions with those he maintained over three decades. At the founding of *Critical Quarterly*, Cox affirmed an idea of 'common culture' which centred on 'great literature', and on an ability to use language with lucidity. Speaking to the Bullock Committee, he warned of the dangers of 'popular culture' for education. Now, his Report, for all its efforts to incorporate aspects of the progressive tradition, does not address the concerns of progressivism's more radical strands: its endorsements of aspects of progressive English teaching so often reach their limits where they begin to touch on cultural relationships and conflicts. The chapter on *Bilingual Children* separates linguistic issues from cultural ones – and does not deal with the latter kind. The discussion on *Equal Opportunities* breaks down where it touches on the relationships between subordinate cultures and school knowledge. The proposals on *Standard English* do not admit non-standard dialects as languages of learning. And the chapter on *Literature* outlines a model of reading which keeps in place the reader's humble relationship to 'great literature' even where it concedes a redefinition of the content of the canon. In each of these areas, there are moves towards acceptance of the tenets of progressive English teaching. But the narrowness of the Report's cultural understandings in each case works to render its discourse on equal opportunity a hollow one. Within the shell of the new discourse, new restorationist meanings are accommodated.

In the sections that follow, I aim to show something of the Report's restorationist content. In this sense, what I write will be a critique. But it can also be read in another way, as an account of the means by which the Report works towards hegemony. 'Cox' recognises, engages with and *modifies* the concerns of English teachers. It is in the *whole* of this three-part process that the nature of its hegemonic project can be understood. To repeat Gramsci's insistence, hegemony is secured by winning not merely the acquiesence but the 'active consent of the governed'. For this to occur, there must be some meeting point between the concerns and interests of subordinate and dominant groups. I have already shown how themes associated with 'modernisation' are a nexus for the National Curriculum of a Conservative government and the reforming programmes of sections of the left. I have also suggested how the political difficulties in which teachers and educationalists now find themselves have contributed to a sense of the necessity of tactical adjustment. Now I want to show the operation of hegemony at a different level, based neither on tactical consider- ations nor agreement merely with the broad sweep of the modernis- ing arguments that justify the National Curriculum. This involves taking the concept of 'revolution/restoration' down to the detail of the Report's arguments. I will try to identify there the ways in which 'Cox' encounters and modifies politically radical traditions, so as bring about elements of valuable change, and at the same time to effect a marginalising of possible alternatives.

A discourse of passive revolution
Class
The relationship between social class and educational achievement was central to post-war educational policy in Britain, and endured as a topic of perceived importance well into the 1980s. It was the main focus of sociological research, a recurring motif in the official reports of the post-war period, a major element in political rhetoric and a prime contributor to arguments for comprehensive reorga- nisation. The general tendency of the period was for the relation- ship between social class and education to be conceptualised in ever-finer detail. The decades which began with statistical enquiry into general patterns of class-related achievement ended with exploration of the micro-processes of classroom relations. One

effect of this shift was a rethinking of many of the key terms of progressive education. Once, they celebrated the growth of essential human qualities through education. In as much as 'class' entered progressive thought it was as the 'other' of education. It connoted the 'industrial', class-divided society outside the classroom – the antithesis of creativity. Increasingly, in the 1960s and 1970s, however, class entered the classroom. 'Experience' and 'language' were seen not simply as essential human attributes, but as qualities whose development occurred in and through social relationships. More awkwardly still – for those wishing the classroom to be a haven from the storms of a divided world – class-focused research began to render problematic the relationship between teachers and learners. The hidden, normative pedagogies of progressive education and the resistances of students were established as new, complicating factors in the study of social class and education.[48] Nor were these issues left only to researchers to investigate. Increasingly, though on a small-scale, they became the focus of a new practical pedagogy,[49] that started from an attempt to understand the 'maps of meaning'[50] with which students operated, and the histories and cultures which contributed to the construction of such maps.[51]

'Cox' forsakes both kinds of enquiry. The large-scale social factors that correlate with educational achievement are as much neglected in the Report as the workings of 'class' within relations of teaching and learning. These very considerable shifts are, of course, enacted in the National Curriculum as a whole; they are not exclusive to 'Cox'. But 'Cox' does not simply translate policy conclusions formulated elsewhere into terms appropriate to English: it has to engage with important traditions within its subject area. It is precisely because the Report engages with these positions, yet concludes by affirming a modified version of the now-dominant viewpoint, that it can be described as hegemonic. In this context, it employs what could be called a tactic of 'half-recognition'. In some senses, the Report accepts 'class' as an important issue: one chapter is devoted to equal opportunities and in another the discussion of Standard English is conducted in terms which are in a sense class-related. But it is that 'in a sense' which marks the problem. Class remains an issue, but it is present in a much weaker form than in recent attempts at critical research and pedagogy. This weakness takes at least three forms. First, and most obvious, is the 'gestural' way in which 'class' as a pre-eminent factor in educational achievement is recognised:

> A strong association between social background and educational attainment is one of the best-documented findings of educational research . . . The causes of such differences are not well understood. But curricular and assessment arrangements should aim to raise expectations, and to help narrow the gap wherever possible.[52]

This reads like the beginning of a chapter on how the curriculum can be reorganised so as to have regard to the class situation of students. The problem is that it is actually the *only* reference to the issue. Teachers are informed of the existence of a problem and told to do something about it. If they wish to find a framework in which they can begin thinking about issues of class and achievement, they are referred to the levels of attainment and programmes of study set out elsewhere in the document; they 'should raise' expectations. We are back here in the DES-land of 'relevant and regardless': 'Cox' assumes that the single set of nationally-specified guidelines will somehow, even though they take no account of the conflict and resistance surrounding the education of working-class students, 'help narrow the gap wherever possible'.

A similar problem concerns the fullness of the Report's understanding of the lives of students. References to dialect, identity, family and community suggest a fairly complete realisation of the experience of students from subordinate social groups.[53] But these references are again little more than gestures: it is the national, official culture which is the subject of Cox's sustained attention; subordinate cultures take a subordinate place in the Report's construction.

Third, there is the conceptualisation of 'class'. It does not signify a *relationship* of possession/dispossession or advantage/disadvantage, whose structure and effects might be studied by students and teachers. Instead, it signifies only *difference*. It is located in the empty space of a 'plural society', that contains social groups of various kinds, and in which poverty or sharp conflict of interests are not issues. This is a point of more than sociological interest. Two understandings – of 'class' as a site of injustice, and of 'class' as a *relationship* between people, the identification of which required skills of abstraction and analysis – have sustained radical English teaching. 'Cox', retaining the term 'class', has emptied it of such critical content, and made it fit for a project of 'passive revolution'.

Language, culture, politics

The Report's treatment of language and culture is subject to the same general contextual pressures as its handling of 'class'. But whereas with class, the Report avoids deep intellectual engagement with the issue, in the case of language and culture it addresses seriously some central questions.

One of the unresolved, but extremely productive, problems of English is the relationship between language and culture. In different ways, each claims a central position, as the nexus of the subject as a whole. 'Culture', in Raymond Williams' usage, denotes a 'whole way of life'.[54] For Richard Johnson the term refers to 'the subjective side of social relations' – the symbolic processes of social life as a whole'.[55] Language would be *one* of these processes, an aspect of culture. The concepts used to investigate other forms of cultural production, including those that relate to conflict and power, would be equally applicable to language.

Language, however, has a status which other cultural forms cannot possess. It is the function on which largely depends our cognitive grasp of the world. It is the prime means of organising and thus making sense of experience. It is through language that higher-order conceptual abilities are developed. In relation to learning, therefore, language can claim a privileged position.[56]

Even so, language cannot cut itself free from culture. As a form of culture, it is a collective, social phenomenon which registers, and enacts, the histories of its users and the pressures of the contexts of its use: in Voloshinov's words, language can never be 'pure thought'; in language there is always 'a struggle between value judgements'.[57]

A programme to raise levels of educational achievement would need, from this perspective, to integrate cultural and linguistic issues. To leave out language would be to abandon the effort to understand and facilitate intellectual development. To forget culture would be to neglect the social nature of learning: that for most students it takes place in a context in which widely differing cultural codes encounter each other, and where knowledge and power are intertwined. It would be to develop a pedagogy which would mistake one particular, dominant, cultural code for the universal language of Reason.

It appears that 'Cox' seeks to integrate linguistic and cultural understandings. Cox's predecessor, the 1988 Kingman Report on *The Teaching of the English Language*, saw Standard English as 'the language which we all have in common . . . a great social bank on which we all draw'. Effacing the social construction of Standard English, Kingman declared that 'it is the fact of being the written form which establishes it as the standard'.[58] In 'Cox', by contrast, Standard English, which takes the central place in the Report's discussion of language and learning, is described on the one hand as the language of 'formal, written communication' and on the other as a 'social dialect'.[59] Up to this point, the Report registers the impact of sociolinguistic theory on educational thinking. But sociolinguistic insights are constrained by older cultural preferences: the difficulties for learning that the 'double nature' of Standard English presents are not elucidated. The Report's emphasis falls heavily on the linguistic qualities and intellectual advantages of the standard form. With mystifying effect, issues of grammar teaching and the development of 'elaborated' codes are presented in the context of learning Standard English.[60] Repeated references to its 'formal, public' nature[61] place it beyond the reach of conflictual social relationships and cultural codes. In the same movement, non-standard Englishes are related to the informal, private sphere. There is no analysis of the linguistic tasks they can or cannot perform. Beyond urging teachers to be 'sensitive' in teaching the standard form to the non-standard user, the Report pays little attention to what actually occurs in that encounter. The total effect is to give Standard English a neutral authority, deriving from its intrinsic strengths rather than its relationship to social power. 'Cox', thus, restructures the model of language which English teachers are to work with. It also changes the status of language study relative to other aspects of English. It is language, not culture, which lies at the centre of the new map of the subject. The shift is an important one; in making it, 'Cox' has cut itself off from much that is valuable in the last 30 years of English teaching.

In the decades after 1960 a cultural focus for English increasingly entailed one or more of the following elements:

1. an insistence on understanding experience socially, in the context of a 'whole way of life';
2. a judgement of the quality of social life and of culture by reference to the 'authenticity' of the experience it fostered, or to

the possibilities it offered for the creation of a common, democratic culture;
3. a positive evaluation of the cultures of subordinate groups as vital and meaningful. Increasingly, from this perspective, the dominant culture's claim to represent 'universal' human experience was questioned. The central principles of that culture – the nature of literary/cultural value among them, and thus the idea of a cultural heritage – were challenged.

Each of these three aspects is played down in 'Cox'. First, there is no (explicit) attempt to construct a social/cultural role for the subject, in the manner of a Leavis or a Williams. Although the Report cites ostentatiously the texts of a radical tradition (Cobbett, Williams) and makes reference to ideas associated with it, it does not in any serious sense establish a coherent critical perspective on cultural or adopt a dissident political role; the opposite in fact: language stands as a marker of unity, in the midst of accentuating conflicts. Although Britain is experiencing a many-sided crisis, deeper than anything in the post-war past, it would not be possible to gather this from the Report.

Second, its relation of English to a 'whole way of life' is weak. In the last two decades there has been a culture boom. In the mid-1980s, in London alone, 250,000 people were employed in the 'cultural industries'. More than 20 per cent of all consumer spending related to 'leisure' provision.[62] The enormous growth in advertising, the investment of companies in the creation of corporate images, the mediatisation of politics and even the increasing concern with the presentation and marketing of self[63] are all aspects of a cultural transformation of great intensity and scope. These are surely developments which a redesigned, culturally-committed English would want to investigate. But apart from a welcome, but not deeply-explored commitment to Media Studies, 'Cox' has little to say about them. Literature – whose status as just one element in a complex pattern of cultural production is now clear – remains the giant in Cox's cultural field.

Third, the Report does not come to terms with popular culture, and in particular with the cultures of subordinate groups. This is partly because of the repeated collapsing of culture into language, of which the chapter on *Bilingual Children* is one example. But the Report is also weak in this area because it does not make use of what has become one of the major contemporary themes of cultural studies – a determination to take readers seriously. Meanings, as many people have argued, do not exist in texts. They are created in readings, in acts of consumption. To realise this point fully would have radical implications for teachers. It would entail a step 'towards knowing about particular groups of people, and their attitudes and stories'.[64] Taking such a step would involve a move into those areas of culture and cultural conflict over meaning into which the working group does not wish to go: the long war fought by its chairman against subcultural incursions into the knowledge-community of the school here takes its toll. A few verbal flourishes about 'cultural identity' aside, the Report's interest in 'culture' remains limited to the *products* of literature and (sometimes) other media; it does not register the experiences of those who make use, or are asked to make use, of them.

Entitlement

Perhaps the most alluring promise of the National Curriculum is 'entitlement': all students, it pledges, will have access to the 'same, good, relevant programmes of study'. For Cox, too, entitlement is an issue – one that NATE thinks his committee has dealt with particularly well.[65] In his lectures at University College, London in 1991, Cox located the committee's work in a double context: not only in the work of English teachers, but also in the dominant trends of contemporary culture. Between these contexts he detected a correspondence. The multi-culturalism of the classroom paralleled the post-modernism of the wider cultural world. Each valued a diversity of experience; but neither was able to escape from a disabling cultural and intellectual relativism. Cox did not want, he said, to replace diversity with a single culture. But he was concerned to negotiate multi-culturalism in such a way as to hold on to prior cultural and intellectual commitments. Without such commitments, which were essential to making citizens out of students, entitlement was impossible. He enlisted in his argument the work of a Marxist writer, the economic geographer David Harvey. In *The Condition of Postmodernity*, Harvey criticises post-modernist philosophy for its rejection of the attempt to make sense of the 'social whole'. 'Post-modernist philosophers', he writes (in a passage utilised by Cox):

> tell us not only to accept but even to revel in the fragmentations and
> the cacophony of voices through which the dilemmas of the modern

world are understood . . . While it opens up a radical prospect by
acknowledging the authenticity of other voices, post-modernist
thinking immediately shuts off those other voices from access to
more universal sources of power by ghettoising them within an
opaque otherness. . . .[66]

For 'postmodernism', Cox read 'progressive and multicultural
teaching'. While the latter's attentiveness to students' experience is
welcome, it mimics post-modernism by developing a curriculum
that deprives students of kinds of knowledge and understanding
that would allow access to 'more universal sources of power'.

Thus far, students of passive revolution will note, Cox and
Harvey – educational conservative and Marxist – march in step.
Cox seems able to call on the support of a well-established socialist
critique of relativism in his attack on core aspects of radical
education. Like Harvey, Cox defends enlightenment traditions of
social enquiry, and insists on the need to understand social
totalities, not celebrate cultural fragments. It is when we ask what
'totality' means for each writer that the differences between them
become plain. For Harvey, post-modernism has us

> actually celebrating the activity of masking and cover-up, all the
> fetishisms of locality, place or social grouping, while denying the
> meta-theory which can grasp the political-economic processes . . .
> that are becoming ever more univeralising in their depth, intensity,
> reach and power over daily life. . . . The rhetoric of postmodernism
> is dangerous for it avoids confronting the realities of political
> economy and the circumstances of global power.[67]

'Totality' means something else for Cox. It is related not to global
power relationships but to national traditions, national identity and
national unity. In his framework, which is also the framework of his
Report, individuals are empowered by being given access, through
Standard English and knowledge of literary tradition, to a national
culture. Thus, for Cox, 'entitlement' is thoroughly intertwined with
'acculturation'; and 'acculturation', in turn, involves initiation into
a version of culture in which the relationships at the centre of
Harvey's concerns are obscured. The language of change returns us,
once again, to the 'restoration' of conservative values. Like 'class'
and 'culture', 'entitlement' is a term that delivers something very
different from that which it promised; its promise is sufficiently

dazzling to appear to some, in times like these, as the true son of Reason.

Back to the future

1976 is a big date in the history of recent educational change. James Callaghan made his Ruskin speech then, and education generally became less safe a place for progressives. 1975 is not such a special year. In small ways, though, it is worth remembering, as the culmination of a period of sharp debate and bold practice in English teaching. The NATE magazine *English in Education* reflected and stimulated this activity. Its first issue of 1975 was entitled *English and the Social Context.*[68] One of its articles, entitled 'Another Country', juxtaposed with now-unfamiliar clarity the working lives of English teachers at Harrow School and at Hackney Downs. Another, by Harold Rosen, took its title from Brecht:

> In the evening when the Chinese Wall was finished
> Where did the masons go? . . .

It concludes like this:

> It is not a matter of asserting that working-class culture is infinitely superior. (Who suggested that anyway? Where? When?) but rather of demonstrating that it is there at all, that it is pertinent to our concerns, that we build on it or build nothing.[69]

The article records a commitment which has endured among English teachers, though now it is semi-clandestine and seldom fully articulated. Its arguments are now remembered through the distorting lens of a collective self-criticism which has become too harsh. The radical English of the 1970s was in some respects pedagogically ingenuous; in others – involving students in school publishing for local communities – it was remarkably bold and successful.[70] Now labelled as culturally relativist, a closer investigation would reveal that it often intended to do much more than rejoice in the particularities of the oppressed. And though misleadingly nostalgic, often, about the solidity of working-class community, it nevertheless proved quick to adapt to criticisms that it neglected issues of race and gender. It is time that teachers of English sought a re-encounter with the concerns of that period. In a way, that is what the next three chapters do. But they seek no simple resumption of earlier themes; they make contact with them across a set of histories that they have no intention of forgetting.

If radical English teachers have learned anything in the last 15 years, it is that 'culture' and 'community' are best not invoked unless in a sense of complexity and conflict. Changes in the composition of the working class have linked with shifts in the understanding of complicating divisions within classes in such a way that 'class' can no longer be understood as a monolith, nor 'working-class culture' in the singular. Nor are teachers now as confident that the channels of communication between the sympathetic, college-educated 'facilitator' and the students of inner-city classrooms are so free of interference that the value of the teacher as 'empowerer' needs little demonstration.

Many teachers have thus learned to doubt. At the same time, they have become aware of the sheer difficulty of organising a process of learning, whether at the level of a single lesson in an unstreamed classroom or of planning a scheme of work. A new level of pedagogical sophistication has developed over the last 15 years, supported not only by psychologies of language and learning, but by an input from literary theory. Thinking of this kind, about genre, narrative and reader reception has contributed more, overall, to the work of English teachers in the last decade than have reflections on class or culture. Of course, the two sorts of work are not irreconcilable; they need, in fact, to be joined together, but the 1980s were not a good time to make the attempt. In the culture of teaching, demands for a particular sort of accountability have increased and elaborate policies for managing, monitoring and inspecting the curriculum have proliferated. Their general background has been a period of trade union defeat and political revisionism of a startling kind. Something was gained in the English classrooms of these years, but much, also, has been lost: in a climate unfriendly to the practical elaboration of socialist commitments, pedagogic developments have become separated from the concerns that had just begun to find articulation 15 years ago.

The chapters that follow in some respects return to earlier themes. They are concerned with relationships of teaching and learning in a context of cultural difference and antagonism. But to understand these relationships, they employ some of the understandings that teachers developed in the later 1970s and 1980s: they draw from traditions of cultural studies and literary theory that

were not available to teachers in the mid-1970s. Their commitments
– to politics of race and class and gender – are wider than those of
their radical predecessors. They are quizzical, in ways many of us
have learned to be, about the places the committed teacher occupies
in these awkward classrooms. But they remained concerned with
English teaching as one part of an emancipatory and combative
politics. They approach the 'Cox Report' as one – important – event
in a wider politics of culture. They move between the decorous
statements of the Report, and the more evident flashpoints of
political and cultural conflict: the Rushdie Affair, the policing of
schools, the fate of William Shakespeare. In doing so, they
recommence an interrupted conversation among those concerned
with English teaching, and suggest a future for the subject beyond
the limits of 'Cox'.

Notes

1. C. B. Cox, *Education, The Next Decade*, Conservative Political Centre
   1981, p. 12.
2. DES and Welsh Office, *English for Ages 5 to 16*, 1989. See also DES
   and Welsh Office *English in the National Curriculum (No. 2)* 1990.
3. C. B. Cox, *Politics and a National Curriculum in English*, 3 lectures at
   University College, London, February 1991; *Editorial, Critical Quarterly*, 32, 1, Winter 1990; *Cox on Cox: An English Curriculum for the
   1990s* (1991).
4. DES consultation document on the National Curriculum, July 1987,
   quoted in K. Jones, *Right Turn: The Conservative Revolution in
   Education*, 1989, p. 96.
5. See Claus Moser, *Presidential Speech to the British Association for the
   Advancement of Science*, 20/8/90; Institute for Public Policy
   Research, *A British Baccalaureat: Ending the Division between
   Education and Training*, 1990.
6. *The Independent* 5 June 1991.
7. For the mid-1991 revival of the right, see 'Afterword' in this volume.
8. The work of David Hargreaves is interesting in this respect. In *The
   Challenge for the Comprehensive School* (1982) he criticised the
   'fashionable concern with improved standards and better links with
   industry as the key educational projects of our age' and called upon
   teachers 'to take a stronger initiative in the design of future reform'. In
   1987, he was one of the first to lend his support to the National
   Curriculum project set out in the Education Reform Bill (*Times
   Educational Supplement* (*TES*) 11 September 1987. Intervening
   between the two positions was Hargreaves' experience of attempting to

introduce radical reform in London schools at a time of teacher militancy.

9. Cox, *Editorial*, p. 1.
10. Ibid., p. 6.
11. A. Gramsci, *Selections from the Prison Notebooks*, edited by Q. Hoare and G. Nowell-Smith, 1971. pp. 105-20.
12. ibid., pp. 119-20.
13. G. di Lampedusa, *The Leopard*, translated A. Colquhon, 1963, pp. 172-93.
14. See, for instance, D. Forgacs, 'Gramsci and Marxism in Britain', *New Left Review*, 176, July-August 1989 p. 82; and E. Hobsbawm, 'Gramsci and Political Theory', in A. Showstack Sassoon, *Approaches to Gramsci*, 1982, p. 29.
15. For an example of Italian trade union responses to fascism see A. Davidson, *The Theory and Practice of Italian Communism*, Volume 1, 1982. p. 293: 'The Fascist regime is a reality and should be taken into account. This reality arises from our principles . . . which have imposed themselves. The union policy of Fascism, for example, in certain regards identifies itself with our own. We were not in agreement with the liberal State because it did not intervene in the economy . . . The Fascist regime has passed a law which is certainly fiery, on discipline in the collective relations of labour. In that law we see accepted principles which are ours as well. While the liberal state lasted . . . and while the workers remained firm in their misunderstanding of the State, a law of such a sort was not a proposition. The Fascist revolution has cut the Gordian knot and we must note that'.
16. D. Finch, 'The National Curriculum Con-trick', in *Socialist Teacher*, 45, Autumn 1990, pp. 22-3.
17. These terms are not, of course, meant literally. By 'revolution' I refer to 'equal opportunity' and 'progressive' traditions of reform. By 'restoration', I mean conservative projects aiming to render the curriculum uncritical and to increase differentiation between groups of students.
18. K. Jones, *The National Curriculum*, in *London Review of Books*, 13, 1 10 January 1991.
19. B. Moon, *A Guide to the National Curriculum*, 1991, pp. 10-14.
20. *TES* 29 March 1991.
21. *TES* 31 May 1991 reports that the Secretary of State for Wales has ordered that the *Wales and Industrial Britain* unit of the National Curriculum in Wales should stop at 1900. Thus the major achievements of the Welsh working class, centring on the South Wales Miners' Federation, are deleted at a stroke.
22. T. Eagleton, *Ideology*, 1991, p. 115.
23. Cox, *Critical Quarterly*, 1990, p. 2.
24. National Association for the Teaching of English (NATE) (R. Bain, B.

Bibby and S. Walton) *The National Curriculum in English for ages 5 to 16: Summary and Commentary on the proposals of the Cox Committee*, p. 29 and p. 8. (The pamphlet is described as a 'personal response' to Cox, though it has all the appearance of an authoritative statement).

25. C. MacCabe, 'Language, Literature, Identity: Reflections on the Cox Report', *Critical Quarterly*, 32, 4 (1990) pp. 10–11.
26. See M. Stubbs, 'Knowledge about Language: Grammar, Language and Society' (Special Professorial Lecture, Institute of Education) 1990.
27. Cox, UCL Lectures.
28. Cox, 'Critical Quarterly: Twenty-Five Years', *Critical Quarterly*, 26, 1 and 2, 1984.
29. Cox and Dyson (ed.) *The Black Papers on Education – Revised Edition* (1971), Introduction, p. 10.
30. Cox, *Critical Quarterly: Twenty-Five Years*, p. 11.
31. Cox and Dyson, op. cit., p. 9.
32. ibid., p. 17.
33. Black Paper 2, p. 26.
34. Cox, *Critical Quarterly: Twenty-five Years*, p. 15
35. R. Boyson in *Education*, 25 January 1991. For an account of Cox's political activity, see C. Knight, *The Making of Tory Education Policy in Post-war Britain 1950–1986*, 1990.
36. Ibid., p. 77.
37. Ibid., p. 100.
38. Cox, *Education: the next decade* p. 12.
39. Ibid., p. 7.
40. Ibid p. 14.
41. Cox, *Critical Quarterly: Twenty-Five years*, p. 15.
42. B. Holmes, preface to *The Search for Common Ground*, Oliver (ed.) for National Council for Educational Standards, 1985.
43. Cox, *The Arts: the Search for Common Ground*, pp. 44–52.
44. Cox, *Cox on Cox*, p. 13.
45. Ibid., p. 4.
46. See 'Cox', Appendix 6. Cox maintained that this material was included at the behest of a conservative supporter on his committee (UCL Lectures).
47. See S. Ball, A. Kenny and D. Gardner, 'Literacy, Politics and the Teaching of English', in I. Goodson and P. Medway (eds) *Bringing English to Order*, 1990. pp 47–86.
48. On the development of the 'new' sociology of education, see Education Group, Centre for Contemporary Cultural Studies *Unpopular Education: Schooling and Social Democracy in England since 1944* (1981) pp. 184–8. For a criticism of progressivism as a normative practice, see

(for example) V. Walkerdine, *It's only natural: Rethinking child-centred pedagogy* in Donald and Wolpe (ed) *Is there anyone here from education?*, 1984. For school-student resistance, see, for example, P. Corrigan, *Schooling the Smash Street Kids*, 1979.

49. See the magazine *Schooling and Culture*, 1977–84.
50. For cultures as 'maps of meaning', see J. Clarke, S. Hall, T. Jefferson and B. Roberts, Subcultures, Cultures and Class in S. Hall and T. Jefferson (eds.) *Resistance through Rituals: Youth Cultures in Post-war Britain*, 1974, pp. 10–11.
51. See P. Cohen, *Really Useful Knowledge: Photography and Cultural Studies in the Transition from School*, 1990; and J. Hardcastle, 'Classrooms as Sites of Cultural Making' in *English in Education*, 19, 3, 1985.
52. 'Cox', Chapter 11, Paragraph 10.
53. 'Cox', 4.32, 4.50, 6.18.
54. R. Williams, *The Long Revolution* (1965), pp. 57–8.
55. R. Johnson, 'The Story so far: and further transformations?' in D. Punter (ed.) *Introduction to Contemporary Cultural Studies*, 1986, pp. 277–313.
56. For these points, see the summary of the place of philosophies of language in English teaching in P.Medway, *English and English Society at a time of Change* in Medway/Goodson, op. cit., pp 1–46.
57. V. N. Voloshinov, *Marxism and the Philosophy of Language* (1986) p. 11 and p. 23.
58. DES, *Report of the Committee of Inquiry into the Teaching of English Language* (1988) para 31, p. 14.
59. 'Cox' 4.32, 4.36, 5.42.
60. Stubbs, one of the authors of the Cox report, comments on its confusion of questions of grammar with questions of Standard English (Stubbs, op. cit., p. 3).
61. For example, 'Cox', 4.35.
62. Greater London Council, *London Industrial Strategy*, 1985, p. 169. *The Guardian* (10 April 1991) quotes a Labour Party estimate that 400,000 people work in British 'culture industries'.
63. D. Harvey, *The Condition of Postmodernity*, 1989, pp. 285–8.
64. M. Green, *Introduction* in M. Green in association with R. Hoggart for the English Association, *English and Cultural Studies: Broadening the Context, Essays and Studies*, 1987.
65. NATE, op.cit., p.19.
66. Harvey, op. cit, pp. 116–17.
67. Ibid., p. 117.
68. *English in Education*, Volume 9, Number 1, 1975.
69. H. Rosen, 'Out there, or where the masons went?', from *English in*

Education, 9.1; reprinted in M.Hoyles (ed.) *The Politics of Literacy*, 1977.
70. See Hoyles, ibid.

Chapter Two
Interrupting the Lecture: 'Cox' Seen from a Classroom

Anne Turvey

The Gustave Tuck Theatre in University College, London, was the venue for Professor Brian Cox's recent series of lectures, *Politics and a National Curriculum in English.*[1] It is no distance at all, as the crow flies, from the Institute of Education's English department, where I work, to University College. But for me it seemed a long walk and curiously unsettling to be back in such a place as a lecture 'theatre': the high hall; the banked rows of seats you slide along; the lectern in relation to which the speaker must arrange himself to establish an attitude, a tone, a particular style of lecturing, and much else besides . . . like classroom teaching really, I mused, but also nothing like it, such a world away, and one I have had relatively few dealings with since I left university in 1973. No interruptions to the lecture, for a start – 'Is this course work or not, Sir?' . . . 'Please, Miss, is this factual or creative?' – no questions from the floor, and certainly no need to tell *us* to get out our rough books and jot down our ideas.

It was a setting which breathed age, calm, seriousness; and we were certainly rather more of a 'captive audience' than I am used to. I spent the time waiting for things to start, in amused contemplation of the inscription behind the lectern:

Remember the Days of Old Consider the Years of Each Generation

In my imagination, I filled the hall with some of the more vivid characters from the 'generation' or so I have taught in schools and to whom I have tried to teach 'days of old'. After repeated readings, soundings over in my head, the inscription had gathered a definite rhythmic quality. I added a musical accompaniment and pretty soon had come up with the Gustave Tuck version of a Pepsi-cola ad.:

rows of third and fourth formers rising to their feet, heads held high and eyes to the future clutching, perhaps, 'Non-statutory Guide lines' and singing about 'one world', 'the hope of our nation' and 'the new generation'. Perhaps, after all, the perfect setting for this lecture, the theme of which was 'literature and the canon'. What better place to explore issues of texts, reading, tradition and change?

The next hour or so was distinctly odd and I have spent some time since trying to define for myself the nature of that oddness. That Professor Cox believes such a lecture, a kind of 'gloss' on the original Report, is necessary now, is interesting in itself. It may well signal a recognition that the responses from teachers after initial publication of the Report, for the most part sighs of relief for all the things it was not – that those responses have altered and darkened in the months since: fewer sighs of relief now; more nervous gulps. Inevitably the demands of the assessment procedures as outlined in the Report have meant that teachers have become caught up in an enormous amount of work and weighed down by record-keeping: sheer exhaustion is surely expressed in some of these reactive gulps.

However, it is other issues which emerged clearly from Cox's lecture and which are woven into the fabric of the written documents that I want to outline here as the starting point for a discussion about teaching, learning and English. These issues concern language and literature and their relationship to learning and above all, to identity.I want to show that how we understand what goes on in classrooms depends upon the theory of learning we work with. This not only affects how we read the Cox Report but, at the risk of telling teachers what they should gulp about, I think it must be the basis for an ongoing debate about English in the National Curriculum. Of course we must continue to question and challenge all those 'key stages' and 'levels' and, indeed, the whole vast framework for assessment. But while we bark up that tree, some alarming things are getting away and breeding deep in the woods.[2]

Cox began with two readings, each highly revealing of his own position, it seems to me. The first was from the novel, *The Remains of the Day*, Kazuo Ishiguro's portrait of an aging butler, Stevens, who has embarked on a motoring trip through the West Country after a life-time spent 'in service'. Stevens' upright patriotism, his naïve views and desiccated life, his loyalty to the late, very clay-footed Lord Darlington – these enlist our pity and our amusement. In the spirit of such an ironic characterisation, Stevens' swelling

hymn of praise to the English countryside (near Salisbury!) as 'the
most deeply satisfying in the world' is funny. Coxread to us from
the section of the novel where Stevens tries to define for himself this
quality in the landscape which, Stevens concludes, is 'probably best
summed up by the term "greatness".'

> For it is true, when I stoodon the high ledge this morning and viewed
> the land before me, I distinctly felt that rare, yet unmistakable feeling
> – the feeling that one is in the presence of greatness. We call this land
> of ours *Great* Britain, and there may be those who believe this a
> somewhat immodest practice. Yet I would venture that the landscape
> of our country alone would justify the use of this lofty adjective.
>   And yet what precisely is this 'greatness'? Just where, or in what,
> does it lie? I am quite aware it would take a far wiser head than mine
> to answer such a question, but if I were forced to hazard a guess, I
> would say that it is the very *lack* of obvious drama or spectacle that
> sets the beauty of our land apart. What is pertinent is the calmness of
> that beauty, its sense of restraint. It is as though the land knows of its
> own beauty, of its own greatness, and feels no need to shout it. In
> comparison, the sorts of sights offered in such places as Africa and
> America, though undoubtedly very exciting, would, I am sure, strike
> the objective viewer as inferior on account of their unseemly
> demonstrativeness.
>   This whole question is very akin to the question that hascaused
> much debate in our profession over the years:what is a 'great' butler?[3]

In the audience we all smiled at the naive celebration and the
ponderousanalogy – Great Britain and Great butlering – and with
Professor Cox's addition of some choice bits from the 1921
Newbolt Report, also hymning the 'greatness', 'glory', 'richness' of
the English language, we were surely meant to feel how far we have
come from Stevens' parochial attitudes. The Ishiguro piece must
have been chosen to make just this point: we are way beyond all
that elegiac, sonorous, sentimental flag-waving and, what is more,
we can laugh at it. It is a multi-cultural world now and that kind of
imperialistic swooning to the strains of Elgar just will not DO. But
this is where things in the Gustave Tuck Theatre got a little odd and
then continued curiouser and curiouser.

Cox went on to read us a poem (he liked reading poetry aloud, he
confided, and he rarely got the chance to do it in a lecture). He read
it in a tone of voice which struck me as precisely elegiac, sonorous
and sentimental, all those things we laughed at in Stevens, the

superannuated butler. The poem was Philip Larkin's *MCMXIV*. It is one of those nation-on-the-eve-of war, unaware-of-impending-doom elegies, a pity-the-society-which-can-never-be- the-same-again poems. Here it is:

MCMXIV

Those long uneven lines
Standing as patiently
As if they were stretched outside
The Oval or Villa Park,
The crowns of hats, the sun
On moustached archaic faces
Grinning as if it were all
An August Bank Holiday lark;

And the shut shops, the bleached
Established names on the sunblinds
The farthings and sovereigns,
And dark-clothed children at play
Called after kings and queens,
The tin advertisements
For cocoa and twist, and the pubs
Wide open all day;

And the countryside not caring;
The place-names all hazed over
With flowering grasses, and fields
Shadowing Domesday lines
Under wheat's restless silence;
The differently-dressed servants
With tiny rooms in huge houses,
The dust behind limousines;

Never such innocence,
Never before or since,
As changed itself to past
Without a word – the men
Leaving the gardens tidy,
The thousands of marriages
Lasting a little while longer:
Never such innocence again.[4]

The sunshine will not last; there is a rustling behind the wainscot-ting, 'dust behind limousines'. Cox said he admired the poem's 'exquisite poise' and recognis ed in it 'that longing we all share for

continuity and a sense of collective identity'. He seemed particularly
moved by the last line; in fact he repeated it:

Never such innocence again.

What on earth was happening here? Where had all the irony gone?
We had just been led away from endorsing Stevens' nostalgic
grandiloquence about Englishness and greatness, 'Englishness as
heritage, as mythical identity',[5] only to be drawn back now, albeit to
a slightly reworked set of touchstones: 'poise', 'continuity', 'tradition', 'safety'. At this point, I really had to fight the urge to put up
my hand and ask several questions. 'Please Sir, what do you mean
by "collective identity"?' for starters. Hadn't we just mocked (some
of us rather more gently and indulgently than others, it would seem)
a particular notion of national unity, one that is not just reflected in
the 'greatness' of the English language, but actually made possible
by it. Hadn't we laughed at this notion as expressed in the Newbolt
Report of 1921:

> The English people might learn as a whole to regard their own
> language, first with respect and then with a genuine feeling of pride
> and affection. More than any mere symbol it is actually a part of
> England; to maltreat it or deliberately to debase it would be seen to
> be an outrage; to be sensible of its splendour would be to step upon a
> higher level . . . Such a feeling for our own native language would be
> a bond of union between classes and would beget the right kind of
> national pride.[6]

It seems I had been laughing with a bit too much relish at this kind
of thing! Perhaps it wasn't a joke after all, or perhaps it was because
I wasn't English and I had missed something.

Momentarily chastened and genuinely puzzled, I really did want
to ask how that 'collective identity' Cox longs for, squares with
what he referred to virtually in the same breath, as 'diversity'. He
made much of the oppositions: continuity and change; unity and
diversity. However it was certainly not as oppositions that they
emerged: reconciliation is the thing. A national curriculum could
do this and, what is more, he told us his own committee had been
guided in their deliberations by a desire to provide children with the
'safety' which a sense of continuity affords. As far as literature in
schools is concerned, the equation goes something like this:

Tradition + X = the safety of collective identity.

The missing 'X' is something called 'range' and it is referred to many times in the Report's statements about literature. At its most exalted level, the term is associated with 'the range of possible patterns of thought and feeling' (7.2) and 'the wide range of feelings and relationships' (7.3) which literature offers, and because of its special relationships with readers, it makes possible self-awareness and personal growth.

After this elevated sense of 'range', Chapter 7 of the Report, the one devoted to Literature, settles down to a consideration of how we select texts to study in schools. Broadly speaking, this amounts to a celebration of breadth: 'The concept of "range" extends also – and very importantly – to social and cultural diversity.' (7.4) Teachers, it was made clear, have a duty to address this question of 'diversity'. In his lecture, Professor Cox spoke of the 'racial tolerance' which would result from studying literature in English from other countries, and this principle is there in the Report as well.[7]

Teachers are encouraged to 'extend the scope', to broaden, to draw in and draw on, all of which suggest a movement outwards from some rock-solid, enduring, central edifice:

> English teachers should seek opportunities to exploit the multicultural aspects of literature. Novels from India or Caribbean poetry might be used for study of differing cultural perspectives, for example. Not only should this lead to a broader awareness of a greater range of human 'thought and feeling', but – through looking at literature from different parts of the world and written from different points of view – pupils should also be in a position to gain a better understanding of the cultural heritage of English literature itself (7.5).

'Exploiting' and 'using' the 'multicultural aspects of literature' sounds a bit like travel: it broadens the mind. But it is definitely *safe* travel: you return to the harbour of 'the cultural heritage of English literature itself'.

To bring into classrooms this 'other' literature is to acknowledge cultural diversity. Simple. Once acknowledged and accepted, the result is an increased understanding and mutual respect among students. 'Safety' for all. A large part of the problem here is in the

understanding of culture upon which such multi-cultural optimism
is based:

> 'Cultures' figure in such explanations as finite and self-sufficient
> bodies of contents, customs and traditions. . . . The 'contents' of the
> other cultures are embraced as part of the narrative of the consensual
> English culture, but without disturbing the norms which define its
> categories, its values, and its patterns of differentiation.[8]

If the norms *are* disturbed, if the central structure is threatened,
well that is a different matter. Who is safe then? This nervousness
and anxiety lie beneath the apparent celebration of 'different'
literature in the Cox Report. They were there in Professor Cox's
lecture when he referred to an article by the poet Stephen Spender,
printed in *The Independent* magazine of Saturday, November 3,
1990. In this article, Spender expressed support for a London A-
level syllabus which included works for study from 'ethnic minority'
writers. Many teachers, Spender wrote, believed that literature
should 'relate to the beliefs and traditions and language' of their
students. I am not here concerned with Spender's understanding of
what the readers in classrooms actually *do* with these texts which
'match' their homes and cultural background, of what it means for
a teacher to study a book with students; rather, what startled me at
the time, and what is pertinent to my argument, is the way Cox
himself had read this article. What struck a chord with him was
Spender's vision of what might happen when 'any agreed standard
supplied by a classical tradition of acknowledged great writers' is
challenged:

> The idea of a future in which there is no single standard but a
> multiplicity of standards, each with its separate variety of correct-
> ness, is indeed terrifying.

Cox repeated the word 'terrifying'. He seemed visibly shaken by
such a prospect: 'chaos is come again'.

Is the 'balance' then, which Professor Cox told us was one of the
Report's most important achievements, something arrived at from
a consideration of the diversity of classrooms as experienced by
teachers and pupils, or is it just a way of calming fears and
smoothing the edges, making safe any alternative or oppositional

views? Clearly, I have suggested that the latter gets closer to Cox's understanding.

So, what view of 'diversity' and 'balance' am I advocating as an alternative? How would I define these terms and their relationship to literature and classrooms? If we think of the cultural diversity of a classroom as involving many different personal histories, then what view of 'balance', which does not bury the sense of individual agency, might describe the activities of that classroom? How might literature and reading organise the sort of learning which takes account of individual paths at the same time as it makes possible a shared activity among students and teachers? The next section of this chapter will address these questions.

Those third and fourth year students I mentioned earlier are becoming rather shadowy figures, stranded in the stygian gloom of the Gustave Tuck Theatre. A classroom then, and some learning of the kind I have referred to. It was, in fact, an A-level class of 10 'Lower 6' students in a girls' school in the east London borough of Newham. We were studying Jean Rhys' novel *Wide Sargasso Sea*. It was the first year this novel had been on the A-level syllabus, an innovation made possible by the changes Stephen Spender referred to in his article. Jean Rhys was one of the authors included in the new 'African and Caribbean Literature' paper.[9] In the lesson I have in mind, we were discussing how to go about a particular essay question invented by me. As it was the first year in which studying this particular novel was possible, there was a certain shot-in-the-dark feeling when it came to thinking about the examination.

I had taught most of these girls for several years. We had studied *Jane Eyre* in the fifth year and this had influenced my choice of *Wide Sargasso Sea*, Jean Rhys' alternative view of Rochester's 'mad' wife. A picture is probably emerging of the kind of 'A' level lesson this was: I chose the texts we studied; I had in mind an examination at the end of the course and the need to prepare 'thoroughly' for it; I introduced discussions around themes which I thought were interesting and 'relevant' but were also 'good bets' for the exam, in short, the 'we' with which I began the description of the lesson, suggests rather more of negotiation and pupil-centredness than was in fact the case. I am sure this picture of an 'A' level lesson is a familiar one to many and I am certainly not apologising for my role in it. At the same time, I am suggesting that the social and cultural relationships which make up classrooms have at their centre questions of diversity which cannot be separated from

questions of power, and which were particularly obvious as this
lesson progressed. Who speaks, who doesn't, who puts the price tag
on a contribution, what ultimately counts as knowledge – these are
not 'outside' the question of what book you are reading, a kind of
background to the lesson; rather, they constitute, at the deepest
level, the kind of learning and identity formation I am looking at.

So what happened? My focus in the lesson was the position in the
novel of Antoinette Cosway, the Creole girl who is 'married off' to
Rochester. Jamaica featured a great deal in our discussion as the
'setting' of the opening section of the story. Jamaica, I probably
said at the time, is lush, tropical, exotic. It is neatly juxtaposed – a
phrase which no doubt appeared later in more than one essay on
'Rhys' use of setting'! – to the cold confines of Thornfield Hall in
England where Rochester takes his increasingly unstable wife and
where the novel ends. Antoinette's sensitivity, her isolation and
feelings of always being an outsider, her brutal treatment by
Rochester and others – these were the main items on my agenda.
Antoinette Cosway was examined as a representative woman,
whose 'tragedy' happens to start in the West Indies. The particular
essay question I had concocted, in the way of such things, was a
quotation from some critic or other, about 'the marooning of the
Creole whites in a landscape where beauty hides cruelty'.

At this point – I had just dictated the essay title – one student
stopped me with a question about the word 'marooned'. Nathalie, a
black girl, was new to the group. I knew she had been born in
Jamaica and had lived there with her grandparents until she was 10,
when she had joined her parents in England. She had come to the
school only in the sixth form and therefore had not been with us for
Jane Eyre; nor had she been 'inducted' into certain practices around
a set text which the others in the group seemed to accept. I started
to explain the word – ' "marooned" means "isolated" or "cut off" '
– but she interrupted impatiently, angrily: 'No, I mean "maroons"
were slaves, weren't they, back home. From Africa and they
escaped to the mountains'.[10]

I remember conceding this angle on the word, but very much in a
spirit of balance and consensus: I was happy enough to have this
new meaning of 'marooned' added to existing ones. I was the
teacher accepting the student's contribution, validating her attempt
to learn the rules of this academic game. Everything the word might
actually mean to her and how she brought to her reading a history
and a personal *lived* experience of being 'marooned' were not really

admitted by me. I was not prepared for Nathalie's sudden resistance – it seemed sudden at the time but now I see it differently – her resistance to the kind of discussion we were having, as well as to my interpretation of a particular word.

'Why', she said to me, 'are we feeling so sorry for Antoinette? Why *shouldn't* she be the outsider there? You just talk as though Jamaica was to blame for her unhappiness, like it drove her mad or something. Anyway, what about all the others? What about Christophine and Tia? They live there. What do you mean "marooned"? I HATE this book'.

I remember trying to shift the ground of our discussion to a consideration of Jean Rhys' life and 'the author's intentions', to themes of exile, loneliness, lovelessness, a woman's place – big 'universal' themes. I was trying to accommodate Nathalie's point of view without really hearing her. Her experiences of separation and exile, of migration from one place to another – Jamaica to West Ham, indeed – did more than just inform her reading of the novel and her understanding of a particular word, although they did these things. She was attempting to make sense of her lived history in the light of a book which she felt marginalised that history, a book which I seemed to endorse. The result of this was her challenge. There was a conflict in the classroom between the authority of a white woman teacher and the resistance of a black student. The book had a meaning for Nathalie which she tried to articulate against the grain of an academic discourse to do with texts and A-level essays and my desire to give these students access to a particular kind of language work and a particular kind of 'literary experience'. I responded to her contribution as to a disruption and I was aware that the other students, several of whom were black and shared some of Nathalie's history, appeared to be on my side!

Learning, in this English lesson, had begun with a student's question about a word – 'marooned'. What developed was a complex negotiation, a struggle in fact, at many levels. Clearly there are considerable inequalities of power here, underlying how we were all positioned, and in schools these structures can often seem overwhelming. In this particular lesson, race was also an issue which determined different readings of the book and what happened around those readings. Nathalie's challenge resulted in a discussion about different races, isolation, leaving home, moving away, which then 'looped' back to the word 'marooned'. By this stage the word had assumed a significance for all of us, a meaning in fact, which would not have been possible as long as I was calling all the shots. Nathalie taking possession of the book in the way she did resulted in something much richer for the group.

I have said that the learning in this episode involved a struggle at many levels. Nathalie comes to define for herself the meaning of a word and to relate that meaning to her own history in ways I could not have predicted or controlled. Furthermore, her inward language development cannot be separated from the social interactions of this particular east London classroom. Language use is active; it is 'behaviour', developed historically and socially and often painfully.

The version of learning I have sketched briefly here has its roots in the theories of Vygotsky. For teachers in classrooms and researchers in education, his work has extraordinary resonance, insisting as it does on the inter-connectedness of language, thought and history. Jane Miller, in her recent book *Seductions*, has written eloquently about one aspect of Vygotsky's theory of learning which throws light on Nathalic's cxpcricncc:

> . . . a theory which entailed a ceaseless struggle for meaning. The individual's struggle progresses by establishing, in communication with other speakers of the same language, what a word *does not* mean. The current meanings of the word 'dog' are learned not by assembling the characteristics of 'dog' which distinguish it from, say, 'sheep', but by winnowing 'dog' out of the clusters of overlapping concepts within the language which are not regarded by adult speakers as essential components of the meaning of 'dog'. Such a theory – developed in opposition to behaviourist explanations of learning and to structuralist theories of mind and language – makes learning, and particularly the learning of self, a process of strenuous and intention-directed activity, mediated by language and performed always within specific social and cultural relations . . . And it follows from this that the learning of identity is also the learning of 'the other' and the 'not-self' as well. The striking difference between such an account and the structuralist one of Lacan is that these are not the arbitrary terms of a binary system, but words learned within a specific material history and saturated with social uses.

The relatively recent rediscovery of Vygotsky's work and of the theory of language developed by the Russian writers Vološinov and Bakhtin allows us to think of the learning of identity through language as brought about in history and within social relations which position the person in relation to specific, though always changing, cultural contexts and practices. Blackness, femaleness, class are not learned as separate abstractions, but together and shiftingly, within settings which mark difference and value inconsistently in relation to those settings. Bakhtin's 'dialogic' view of language reminds us that language is learned within actual conversations rather than as a system abstractable from its primary oral uses, and it is a rare conversation which is not internally unsettled by the inequality of its participants. Age, size, gender, class, authority: these are not the context of conversation, they are its organising principles.[11]

I have described one lesson in detail and at length in order to reveal some of the 'cultural contexts and practices' which Miller refers to and to show how identity is formed in relation to them. 'Blackness, femaleness, class' are gathering a dense texture of meaning for Nathalie which are not the same for me or for the other students in that lesson, but at the same time it is the lesson which helps to make possible the learning of those meanings, the learning, I am arguing, of identity.

Studying literature in schools, reading books with students (Jane Austen as much as Chinua Achebe) – these activities are very much a part of the learning 'practices' which concern English teachers. But it should be clear that the classroom is not a neutral environment in which words, meanings, concepts, knowledge in fact, can be straightforwardly handed over, even 'given access to': Nathalie's experience makes it clear that the learning does not happen like that. Furthermore, what gets lost in so many of these arguments about continuity and literary tradition is what lies at the heart of Nathalie's learning in the dynamics of the classroom. The ways in which talk and writing about a text are being developed here in this particular classroom must be seen as social and historical in origin. The discussion about language is an aspect of the culture of the classroom where 'culture' is not that 'finite and self-sufficient [body] of contents, customs and traditions'[12] but rather, culture is something produced, something built up over time by those individuals.

In a recent article focusing on the cultural dimension of classroom learning, Tony Burgess and John Hardcastle draw attention to the place of 'difference' in this view of culture:

> As teachers, as long as we continue in our thinking to abstract language from its context in culture and history and to think of it just as language, or as skills, or predominantly a matter of forms, we shall restrict our view of pupils' learning. We shall not attend

adequately to the difference which lies in classrooms, whether of class or ethnicity or culture or gender. It is necessary to be specific.[13]

To speak of a multicultural education without regard for the ways such 'specifics' as race or gender or class constitute the learning processes, is more than just to miss the point: it empties 'difference' and 'diversity' of all the force and validity of Nathalie's position. Her challenge forced a recognition of difference which involved the individual subjectivities of all concerned and a moving to centre stage of the very issues which Cox's view of 'balance', 'unity', 'shared cultural information' cannot address. The significance of any text studied in class lies largely in those meanings which are constructed among teachers and students in 'active, committed and shared classroom encounters'.[14] Questions of literary merit – which texts ought we to study in school – are the ones which grab the headlines, but these are surely less important than a consideration of the ways texts focus and organise learning in classrooms.

Nathalie's experience offers a cultural perspective on classrooms and learning. That experience involved negotiation certainly but not negotiation which amounts to a fantasy of cooperation and consensus of the sort Professor Cox imagined for us. Nathalie's 'difference' remains central to the way in which she is able to understand a book and claim an expertise in this British classroom.

In various ways the authors of this book are arguing that reading, studying literature and learning about it, are activities which really matter. But surely, we would insist, the connections among these activities – reading, studying, learning – are as complex, rich and specific as Nathalie's experience demonstrates? Furthermore, against such a perspective, how threadbare seems a view of literature teaching, tethered to notions of high culture and elevated feelings which can be, or ought to be, made known to children so that they can somehow respond.

This view lurks in the Cox Report and has found a doughty champion in the person of Martin Dodsworth, chair of the English Association and panellist on 'The Late Show'.[15] In a recent article in the *Times Literary Supplement*, 'The undermining of English: How the National Curriculum threatens literature teaching',[16] he begins uncompromisingly:

The teaching of English literature in British schools is in a mess. It has been in a mess for some time, and it is getting worse.

Pausing, I imagine, just long enough to feel the bracing wind from all those heads, nodding furiously in agreement, he goes on to defend 'great literature' for the insights into the past which it offers students:

> That past is worth knowing about; just to give sixteen-year-olds an inkling of the fact that great literature gives easy and direct access to a world that *was* ours is worth it. . . .

This past and the 'easy and direct access' to it must be protected, preserved, handed on. Teachers are like National Trust custodians, gate-keepers indeed. The texts which make possible a process he calls 'exploring one's own culture' are of a particular, superior, old, 'hard' sort:

> it transpires that at present many students study very little that a person with some literary understanding would regard as precisely, 'English literature'.

It is not clear which bit all these students, and of course their teachers, are getting wrong – the Englishness of the literature, or the literariness of the English. Nor is it clear what Martin Dodsworth's brand of 'literary understanding' amounts to, but I am fairly confident that Nathalie's is the 'wrong' sort! And what of the texts themselves which produce the 'right' sort of literary understanding? Well, Dodsworth's lists of 'proper' authors might appear daunting but the teaching and learning he imagines certainly sound straightforward, largely a matter of choosing the right books:

> English literature offers fifteen and sixteen-year-olds the chance to develop their mastery and understanding of the language in relation to their own feelings and developing attitudes to life. Children in British schools *ought* [Dodsworth's emphasis] to have the chance of *that direct imaginative experience* [my emphasis] that is there for them in Defoe and Swift, Sheridan and Goldsmith, Dickens and the Brontës.

So *that's* where Nathalie and I went wrong: we made such hard work of the whole business! And it seems I didn't choose the right, literary 'double-acts'.

For Dodsworth, what little hope there is to be found in these parlous times lies in the Working Party's 'two recommendations of

substance', the ones about 'pre-20th century writing' and 'some
experience of the plays or poetry of Shakespeare'. Otherwise, the
prospects are, well, 'terrifying'. The mess will get worse still.

Little in the Cox Report's statements about literature is as
crudely high-brow or as far removed from the realities of teaching
and learning as are Martin Dodsworth's pronouncements. But his is
a view which has a strong following among those 'stop the rot'
defenders of a particular kind of national culture which cannot
make sense of Nathalie's position unless making sense involves
accommodation and absorption. This view of identity in relation to
something called culture *is* there in 'Cox', and should be resisted.

Dodsworth has set himself up to lay bare the shortcomings, as he
sees them, of the provisions for English in the National Curriculum:
he is no friend to 'Cox'. So what of 'Cox's' supporters? After all, by
your friends shall they know you. Colin MacCabe has recently
praised the 'brilliance and innovative nature' of the Report's
discussion of language and nationhood, its 'new definition of
national identity'.[17] His pronouncements, in the *Critical Quarterly*
and the national press, have startled and unnerved many who
remember him as the persecuted, young Cambridge radical, tarred
and feathered by anti-structuralists and run out of town on the rails
of stuffy and reactionary academic prejudice. A decade later he
writes in *The Independent on Sunday* of how, driven by 'rage', he
'pulled [his] children out of the state system', snatched, just in the
nick of time it seems, from something pretty nasty. His 'rage', he
says, stems from the 'failure' of the 'comprehensive experiment' and
the 'nonsense of mixed-ability teaching'. He warns the Labour
Party that they have no hope of offering 'a vision of a better world'
until they can properly acknowledge 'different levels of achievement' and put back into their rhetoric the vital missing word. That
word, MacCabe says, is 'results', and teachers should be rewarded
'in terms of results'.[18]

Four months later the editorial in the same Sunday newspaper
took up the rallying cry – 'Results!' – in its own call to arms:
'Parents' rights, children's hopes'.[19] The word 'results' hammer-
blows its way through this leader, part of an enthusiastic welcome
to national testing and all those lost opportunities which can now
be regained. Of course, MacCabe is not responsible for the
anonymous editorial views, but there is a remarkably similar feel to
these pieces, especially in the note of crisis struck which rises to a
swelling chorus of 'tragedy' in the later piece. It is a crisis of falling

standards in literacy and numeracy from which MacCabe must rescue his children; the nation's children will be delivered by the testing. Haunted he may be by the ghosts of his past when he 'skipped school [to] canvass full-time for a Labour victory', but a man's gotta do. . . .

Although MacCabe's celebration of certain things in 'Cox' can properly be seen in the context of these other recent pronouncements, his support is not simply a question of betrayal or a failure of ideological nerve when the whole education thing got rather too close to home: it is more complicated and more interesting than that. He both misreads, in important ways, what 'Cox' is saying about relationships of learning in terms of the cultural 'differences' experienced by children in schools, and he reads other things 'correctly' but does not see how the Report 'stops short'.

MacCabe's enthusiasm stems from what he sees as the Report's grappling with the issue of the standard language, 'at the core of the report'. He praises the ways 'Cox' appreciates both the varieties of English and its attachment to a standard. Furthermore he is heartened by the way 'Cox' seeks to integrate certain linguistic and cultural understandings. But the problems lie precisely here, in MacCabe's misreading of the core of the Report, in his misunderstanding of what the integration amounts to. He underestimates the importance and authority which 'Cox' attaches to the standard form. Other forms, dialects, languages other than English in effect, do not carry the same formal, public weight as Standard English, and despite some nods to the *linguistic* equality of many of these other forms, the reasons *why* there is a contest around language use are not explored. All questions of power and status, whose voice is heard, and what it means to 'teach' (since children 'must learn') the standard form to non-standard users, – these questions become ones of context and register:

> Where it is appropriate to use the standard you use it but there are many uses where other forms, or other languages, are as appropriate.[20]

These 'many uses' for non-standard forms or other languages are not analysed in any of the significant ways they relate to power and prestige. The pre-eminence of the standard form is not challenged. The unthreatening and egalitarian feel to words like 'register', 'appropriateness', 'context' in 'Cox's' discussion of Standard

English has seduced MacCabe. To call a form of language a 'social dialect', as 'Cox' does, without attending seriously to the social standing of that dialect is to severely limit the discussion. 'Cox' fails to address these relationships among language form, the histories of its users and the multiple pressures of the context of its use. The development of language in social relationships and the struggles involved in these relationships – these questions are pushed to one side. In effect, 'Cox' writes out the cultural dimension of language and learning. 'Difference' remains a question of linguistics and the cultural/political issues which the debates around dialect and 'second' languages should highlight, are just not there. This is how 'Cox' works to integrate the linguistic and the cultural, why the result can appear 'safe' to Professor Cox, and why MacCabe feels 'it is difficult to praise too highly the Report's discussion of language':[21]

> If the Report stresses the plurality of voices that make up this island,
> if it breaks the equation of language and the printed word, it insists
> on a common tongue which we must all speak and write.[22]

MacCabe acknowledges that there *are* questions of possession and dispossession when it comes to those groups 'who use dialects or other languages'. They are cut off from 'the language of citizenship'. For sure he sees problems in any attempts to advantage such groups: the 'Cox' project is mightily ambitious: 'Effectively it demands that teachers make all their pupils bi-dialectal in English'.[23] This would be very difficult, he argues, partly because 'teachers by and large do not have the linguistic knowledge'. More seriously (well I think it is more serious but then I can see that the shortcomings of teachers are always good copy) such teaching, assuming teachers could manage it, might 'devalue the local dialect or the home language, as one insists on the primacy of standard for all the most socially valued practices'. What kind of problem is this for MacCabe? Remember that he locates the 'brilliance and innovative nature' of the Report in its discussion of language. He goes so far as to declare it 'far in advance of linguistic theory and pedagogic practice'. Those terms – 'linguistic' and 'pedagogic' – are the key to understanding his perspective, and here he *has* understood 'Cox' correctly: indeed, he shares its limitations. The whole 'problem' is presented in terms of a project of instruction, of school-based remedial activities, where children are seen as worked upon by properly trained teachers to help them master the national, official language and culture.

What about the fullness of students' lives and the part which language plays in their relationships to home and community? 'Cox' does not begin to address these cultural questions and MacCabe's welcoming salute depends on a similar misreading. The exclusions and omissions of the Report's treatment of language and culture have been pointed out repeatedly by those working with bilingual and ESL children. They have recognised that the Report *does* support the idea that bilingual children might know a great deal about language:

> Many pupils are bilingual and sometimes biliterate, and quite literally know more about language than their teachers, at least in some respects (6.11).

However, this affirmation comes, revealingly, from the chapter on *Knowledge about Language*. What an asset such children could be! In Chapter 10, *Bilingual children*, the position is less hopeful. Supporting bilingual children in the mainstream classroom is encouraged, but what end? Here is the Report:

> The implications are therefore that, where bilingual pupils need extra help, this should be given in the classroom as part of normal lessons and that there may be a need for bilingual teaching support and for books and other written material to be available in the pupils' mother tongues until such time as they are competent in English (10:10).

What has happened to these children's linguistic competencies? A case of mainstream asset-stripping? In a recent article in *Language and Learning*, Helen Savva argues it thus:

> It would appear that resources which reflect linguistic diversity should be made available only to bilingual children and then only to those bilingual children who are in need of extra help. In addition, these resources should be withdrawn when bilingual children become competent in English. This is transitional, not full bilingualism. It is not the development and mutual enrichment of two or more languages and cultures but the idea that development must involve the eventual supremacy of one language and the neglect of others.[24]

There is no escaping it: the standard form is always to be our goal, dominant for reasons which go far beyond questions of 'appropriateness'. As with other non-standard forms, other languages are not recognised as languages of learning. So when MacCabe enthuses about the achievement of 'Cox' in removing all the transcendental justifications for the use of the standard form, I am not persuaded that he has put children and the cultural dimension of their learning into his reading of the Report.

Professor Cox, Dodsworth, MacCabe, Prince Charles, Sir Claus Moser – experts to a man. They have all had a turn at the lectern, telling teachers and parents and occasionally even children, what is best for them. It is important to respond to this public debate and I am glad so many of us keep doing so. But there is also a certain weariness in me: at times I don't want to listen to them any more; I'd rather talk to Nathalie.

Her voice and the voices of other students can so easily get lost in accounts which claim to speak for them. So, released at last from the Gustave Tuck Theatre, I propose to listen to some third-year girls talking about their reading and writing. They speak with passion, conviction and above all, knowledge, about the books they choose to read. They are proud of the way they can imitate their favourite authors in their own writing, and their confidence in talking to me about all this seems to chime nicely with many of those trumpeted ideals in 'Cox':

> It is important that teachers should help pupils in this process [their development as writers] by recognising the interrelatedness of writing, reading and speaking and listening. (17.16).

But – a small serpent in paradise and the sort to give Martin Dodsworth a nasty shock: the girls who speak here are defining themselves as readers and writers in relation to a particular genre – romance fiction – and a specific type of this fiction: Mills and Boon novels. Their 'enjoyment' and 'straightforward pleasure' (7.3) exist to a large extent outside the literary practices of school as they understand them, but they talk openly and enthusiastically to me about their reading and are keen to show me their own version of a romance.

Many of the girls I taught read 'masses' of romances and re-read their favourites many times. They buy from junk shops and jumble sales – 'We know who has the best ones for books' – and they swap with others in the third year. Their mothers and sisters are fans and the girls use their local libraries. There is also a second-hand shop in the area which operates a kind of cut-rate lending system. 'They've got boxes and boxes but we know what we're after', one girl told me. The girls are familiar with 'the look' of the books and have developed a strategy for selecting 'a good read':

> It's the cover. See if they're smiling I think it would be a better book – happier. Well, they're all happy really, that part's the same. I mean, that's how it works – you know the ending. But the stories are different.

Two of the girls I spoke to, Caroline and Rebecca, admire a particular author, Penny Jordan, because, they say, her heroines are different from those of some other Mills and Boon writers. Here is Rebecca's reply to my invitation, 'Give me a typical heroine of Penny Jordan':

> Sophisticated and she's quite witty . . . but her best books are when – I think they're quite funny 'cos the man always gets the better – that's the idea but she can get her own back – well you know she will.It's in the dialogue. . . .

It is literary conventions they are telling me about – heroines and dialogue. The girls understand how the 'plot' (their term) progresses towards the ultimate happy ending through a series of misunderstandings and confrontations between the hero and heroine, as the heroine tries constantly to understand the behaviour of the man:

> *Caroline*: They don't know they love each other.
> *Rebecca*: See he does things . . . and she can't understand.
> *Caroline*: Yeah . . . well *you* know they love each other but . . . but.

The girls are quite clear about how the reader knows more than the protagonists and so is in a privileged position. They are articulate about narrative point of view, how the characters are presented to the reader and how this positions the reader in a particular way. Again, they single out Penny Jordan, this time for the way she presents the hero:

> *Rebecca*: The way the hero is described, you *know* he's the hero. . . .
> *AT*:   Because the heroine is attracted to him?

> *Rebecca*: Well she *will* be but that's not what I mean. . . .
> *Caroline*: When he first comes in it's like you're seeing him too . . .
> like the heroine . . . you're seeing him.
> *Rebecca*: Penny Jordan sometimes gives you the view of the man and
> in most romances they're from the woman's point of view
> and once in a while they change back and he's thinking
> something – it's not very often and not many others do
> that.

Rebecca and Caroline's enjoyment, a key 'Cox' term, and a steady diet of the genre have enabled them to 'crack the code' of the romance and this knowledge gives them a sense of power, in relation to the books and in conversation with me: they are the experts here, informing me, a rare enough position for students to be in, for it to merit the closest attention. Our discussion ranged over a number of the genre's conventions – setting, dialogue, rivals, obstacles to the lovers' eventual union and, most enjoyably, 'how far can you go in the physical bits' – and always there is this bounce and verve in what they say. They see themselves as readers and can discuss that position. They understand absolutely the constructed-ness of texts and a large part of their pleasure derives from this understanding. They come to a new romance, expecting it to conform to certain conventions, and their literary competence, 'a sense of how to read', is developing.

I have laboured this point – what the girls know about how the novels work – as a way of answering so many of the critics of the romance text who have not known quite what to do with such books and so have found it difficult or problematic to account for the reader. In much of the critical commentary on romance there is an underlying ambivalence towards the material and the readers. The critic has not wanted to adopt an élitist position which condemns the reader as a passive consumer of mass culture, but at the same time has been reluctant to endorse the literature itself. Even when the readers of romance were shown to be anything but passive or mindless, they have remained, at least in relation to the romance, strangely inert, weighed down by the text. In the case of teenage girls, the readers emerge as vulnerable, impressionable, in need of the teacher's critical armour to fend off the dangers of these texts, dangers which can usually be reduced to various versions of 'Read the book; now live the life'.

With Caroline, Rebecca and their friends there is a markedly different feeling to what they say about the books they choose to read and the stories they most enjoy writing. There are of course clear traces in their writing of the many things they have read, watched, listened to; but what is interesting to me is the way the writers have taken hold of these various voices in fashioning their own. I see this as an activity, not in the spirit of 'exploitation' as suggested by Cox (7.21), a teacher-led mountaineering expedition, 'beginning with writers who are easily accessible' as a 'way into' things wider, higher or deeper, but an activity, the meanings of which the girls are becoming aware of and coming to define for themselves. It is not particularly helpful to think of their commitment to Mills and Boon, either in terms of the novels' formulaic plots or stereotypical characters or even as 'a love of reading for its own sake' (7.19) which can be left alone to mature into something different, something better. What *is* helpful to our understanding of what reading might mean to those we teach, is the ways in which the girls' enjoyment of the Mills and Boon novels connects with a range of reading strategies, a depth of knowledge about the genre and a confidence in talking to me about their enthusiasm. When Helen, a fifth-year student, said to me during a discussion of Jane Austen's *Pride and Prejudice*, 'I love this book: it's just like a Mills and Boon! I mean, the way we know what Elizabeth and Darcy *don't* know. That's in Mills and Boon. I love that!' I was pleased, *not* because this enthusiasm showed she had moved on from a youthful phase to what 'a person with some literary understanding would regard as, precisely, "English literature".' Of *course* I was pleased this student liked Jane Austen: I like Jane Austen, rather a lot in fact, and that was one reason I chose to read *Pride and Prejudice* with Helen's class. I think Jane Austen is 'great'; I do not think Penny Jordan is anywhere near great.But that issue of value is not really the point, any more than it was when Nathalie said, of *Wide Sargasso Sea*, 'I *hate* this book'. Compiling lists of 'really fine authors' (17.16) or debates about 'works . . . of sufficient substance and quality to merit serious consideration' – such parlour games – 'who's in, who's out' – will no doubt continue to entertain: 'Jane Austen – definitely; Jean Rhys – a bit?; Penny Jordan – you must be joking!'. However, my interest in Nathalie's dislike of a book, in Helen's comment and in Caroline and Rebecca's enthusiasm might connect with how I, or others, rate the texts they are reading – but it doesn't *start* there. Any definition of 'precisely "English literature" ' cannot be the 'Everest' in our classrooms for young readers. Of course it is *there*, just as Standard English is there, but they do not constitute the kind of totalising discourse which 'Cox' presents.

Something similar holds true when it comes to these girls' writing and how a teacher might respond to it. The writing of romances which the girls were engaged in was done in their own time, outside the classroom. They showed me the outline for one which they thought was 'just like the real ones', and it was presented with an illustrated front cover and a back-cover blurb. They included all the preliminary pages of the original paper back, including the disclaimer, 'All the characters in this book have no existence outside the imagination of the author and have no relation whatsoever, etc., etc.'.

It is clear that they saw themselves as 'real' writers and the task they had set themselves was to reproduce the conventions of the genre. They wrote eight chapters, in outline form, but pointed out to me that, 'This is cheating really : it should be ten chapters for a proper *Mills and Boon*', and that although these were outlines, not complete chapters, I should realise that, 'We could make it 187 pages if we wanted to, but anyway, Miss, you'll get the idea'. Here then is the outline for the opening chapter of their romance, *Artist's Impression*, typed from their hand-written original but otherwise as they gave it to me:

Chapter 1.

Anne Richards, journalist and part-time painter, is with her office associate, Steve White, at a galery in east New York, cool pale colours, dim lights, and low voices, where Anne is exhibiting a recent painting. A stranger approaches Anne, he's about 6ft 3″ with sandy hair, a muscular build and roguish good looks. He stands behind her and inspects the painting next to Anne's. He is wearing a smart pair of jeans with a short sleeved T-shirt just right for the temperature where as Anne is hot in the expensive, once-in-a-lifetime, wool suit bought with the money from a previous painting. As he comments on the painting she catches the scent of his colonge and turns to regard him. She is instantly struck by his strength and masculinity but as he looks down at her she quickly returns her attention to the painting. They move on together. As they reach Anne's painting the stranger finds himself looking at a young boy playing, on the beach, with a bucket and spade and is amazed at the similarity between the woman he is with and the child. Realising the connection a boyish grin creaps into his features.

"I don't like it! The light is wrong and the whole scene is quite ridiculous."

Anne, appauled by the unsensitivity, begins to defend her painting but later leaves to join Steve for a celebratery dinner.Totaly ignoring her companions request for a date.

Believe me, it really is all there in this opening chapter, not just the authentic sound of the Mills and Boon text, but the ways the girls direct the reader to read their story. This is done with considerable confidence and flair based on an understanding of what they themselves have read, an understanding I want to highlight in relation to their writing.

Their 'romance', a term the girls used consistently rather than 'love story', opens:

at a galery in east New York, cool pale colours, dim lights and low voices, where Anne is exhibiting a recent painting.

What such a gallery might be like 'in real life' – who goes there, how you get your works exhibited, what a painting might actually cost – does not bother them at all, any more than it would a Mills and Boon reader. All they're interested in is a certain cosmopolitan ambience and we identify that immediately. From the semi-precise location – *east* New York! – to the carefully chosen descriptive phrases which signify the world of art, sophistication and money, it is clear what Caroline and Rebecca are doing with the 'setting' convention. They have been able to draw upon their stock of such descriptions to set up a whole network of reader expectations about the milieu and its clientele. This can only be done if you are aware that there are rules to follow, that you are writing within the conventions of a particular genre.

The three main characters – Anne Richards, the heroine, Steve White, her office associate and the mysterious, unnamed hero – these are superbly handled. Steve White, for example, is a minor but significant character and that is how we read him. He is there as a foil for the handsome stranger and the reader knows this at once. He is the third party, on the periphery of Anne's thoughts, a comfortable, well-known dinner-companion, against whom the enigmatic stranger is cast. The reader is invited to speculate about how Anne might be tempted later in the story by such a supportive friend as things develop in a fiery, unpredictable way with the

stranger. Steve is introduced to serve a function and we are not
'taken in' by his niceness. He is part of the genre and the writers
ensure that we read him that way.

The hero is introduced with equal flair. He is nameless, mysterious and forceful:

> A stranger approaches Anne, he's about 6ft 3″ with sandy hair, a
> muscular build and roguish good looks.

True to form, his height and powerful physique, his 'roguish good
looks' are balanced by 'a boyish grin', the perfect Mills and Boon
combination of strength and vulnerability. Furthermore, the
language here – 'roguish good looks' and 'boyish grin' – is very
much a literary one, a product of the genre.

The description of clothes, so often a red herring in teenage girls'
stories, a way for them to dress a character to make him accord
with some model of current fashionableness or good looks – there is
none of that in *Artist's Impression*:

> He is wearing a smart pair of jeans with a short- sleeved T-shirt, just
> right for the temperature whereas Anne is hot in the expensive, once-
> in-a-lifetime wool suit bought with the money from a previous
> painting.

The description has a specific job to do in setting up the relationship between the hero and heroine. His jeans and T-shirt, 'just right
for the temperature', establish him as casual, at ease, in contrast to
poor Anne's over-dressed discomfort.

With the heroine's clothes, as well, the girls show their knowledge
of the literary originals.The phrase – 'the expensive, once-in-a-lifetime wool suit' – tells the reader a great deal about Anne's youth
and inexperience, her financial position and her artistic potential
(the money for the suit has come from the sale of a previous
painting). Most tellingly, it is a phrase straight from a book : it
certainly does not feature in the 'real life' speech of these West Ham
girls! In taking on the literary style of the genre, the girls have
learned how to direct the reader to which details matter in the
descriptions. To adopt such a style is to understand profoundly
'point of view' and a character's relationship to the reader. The girls
manage 'point of view' in an extremely confident way. Our sym-
pathies are, of course, with Anne, the heroine, and at first we see

things, specifically the stranger, through her eyes: 'A stranger approaches Anne, he's about 6ft 3″ with sandy hair, a muscular build and roguish good looks'. But as he 'stands behind her and inspects the painting next to Anne's', there is a shift to accommodate his curiosity about the painting itself, as well as a new angle on Anne. This is quite deliberate and again it is based on their knowledge of the genre. They referred specifically to this in our earlier discussion:

> *Rebecca*: Penny Jordan sometimes gives you the view of the man and in most romances they're from the woman's point of view and once in a while they change back and he's thinking something – it's not very often and not many others do that.

In their story, the shift allows the girls to arouse our curiosity about the young boy in Anne's painting and we perceive the connection at the moment the hero does – the boy is Anne's son! The knowledge gives to his rude criticism of Anne's painting, a pointed humour which the girls consider such an important part of their enjoyment of the Mills and Boon dialogue:

> *AT*: So you like the dialogue to be. . . .
> *Rebecca*: A sort of conflict . . . but funny.

Realishing the connection a boyish grin creaps into his features.

'I don't like it! The light is wrong and the whole scene is quite ridiculous.'

Anne, appauled by the unsensitivity, begins to defend her painting but later leaves to join Steve for a celebratery dinner. Totaly ignoring her companion's request for a date.

The reader has 'rejoined' the heroine's perspective to see if and how she will retaliate. This aspect of the heroine's personality was essential for their enjoyment of a Mills and Boon and a quality they admired in Penny Jordan's books:

> Rebecca: Sophisticated and she's quite witty . . . but her best books are when – I think they're quite funny 'cos the man always

gets the better – that's the idea but she can get her own back
– well you know she will. It's in the dialogue.

In *Artist's Impression* the whole frisson of the encounter between
hero and heroine is pitched at exactly the right level, and to be able
to direct the reader so skilfully, where to look and through whose
eyes, shows a remarkable command of the genre in these 13-year-
old writers. It could be argued that much of the writers' pleasure
and enjoyment, their control and use of literary stylistic features are
acknowledged by 'Cox'. In Chapter 7, *Literature*, in the section
headed 'Approaches to literature' we find this:

> Pupils should be encouraged to respond to all forms of literature in
> ways which they find pleasurable, and hence are likely to promote
> understanding. Their response should be stimulated through a range
> of active strategies. For example, imitation of a writer's use of
> language involves an active response that requires the pupil to make
> meaning yet to show a grasp of the original author's craft at the same
> time (7.20).

Doesn't that pretty well account for Caroline and Rebecca's
practices? Hardly. For a start, what these girls are up to when they
read and write romances is very much *not* part of that whole
reductive framework of imperatives – 'shoulds','oughts', 'musts',
'will be taughts' – which underpins 'Cox', a deeply embedded
network of literary value and hierarchies which wraps students and
teachers and classrooms in a cocoon of assessable levels. It is not
that Caroline and Rebecca's activities cannot be accounted for by
such levels: the accuracy and authentic style of their writing are
indeed impressive and I have no doubt I could find the right slot for
it in the various Attainment Targets. But its significance for the
writers and for any teacher is much more than that and is to be
looked for partly in all those complex social relationships central to
education. How are these two girls positioned in relation to their
families, to each other, to their all-girls' school in east London, to
the English classroom and crucially, how does their writing relate to
these questions, questions which ought to be central to this soi-
disant 'national' curriculum? Caroline, a black girl who shares some
of Nathalie's personal history, reads widely outside the romance
genre; Rebecca, who is white, does not. I can negotiate around such
considerations in my 'assessment' of their writing, just as the girls

do when they write. But they interest me and inform the work I might do with this class around the subject of romance.

Such work would take account of what I know of other reading and writing activities in which Caroline and Rebecca are engaged and the relationship of their 'romances' to these. In a conversation with them after they showed me *Artist's Impression*, I asked, 'Would you write a story like this in English? I mean, what about . . . what do you write in school?' Rebecca replied: 'Not really – it's not the kind of story you do for Miss X. I mean . . . well . . . I write about myself a lot . . . like memories or my opinions . . . or things that happen to you like 'A Visit to the Dentist' but it doesn't have to be true'. Caroline elaborated: It's ok . . . I mean I quite like writing . . . but I mean you sort of know . . . you write . . . you give Miss what she wants . . . I mean I know what she likes'. Rebecca said, 'Or it's like a situation . . . I mean like we're doing this homework . . . it's a letter to the council so they won't close the playgroup in Canning Town. And you have to be a mother and argue . . . well not rude, but persuade them'. What emerges here, instantly familiar to teachers, is the ways reading and writing practices are built up over time within the school context. Caroline and Rebecca are constructing models for their school writing, its intended audience and the appropriateness of its tone, or to put it another way: 'matching style to audience and purpose', and here I'm quoting the Attainment Target sub-heading for *Writing*, a bold, blackly-typed one. This process involves the girls in some pretty impressive skills: sizing up Miss X's preferences and attempting to influence Newham Council, to name but two! The position of personal writing in school and the role of the autobiographical mode are things which English teachers have been active in fostering. Caroline and Rebecca are concerned to sort this out for themselves and have obviously given some thought to the sleights of hand sometimes required to make this and other sorts of writing 'ring true'. They did not seem to resent this frequent invitation by their teacher to examine their own experiences and use them as a coming-to-knowledge of the self which underpins much autobigraphical writing in school. There are models, forms, ways to tell your 'personal' story, just as there are for the romance and the girls are keen to get these right.

Writing, in school and out, is involved in the ways gender is constructed. It seems likely that a teacher would want to explore with Caroline and Rebecca links between the autobiographical and the romance genres which are, on the surface, such different modes. Both forms offer the writer opportunities for reflection and critique, as well as a sense of independence and control. 'Writing', Caroline said to me, 'well, we do all sorts and I like some of it. It's good, too, when you know you're getting better at it. Well, *I* think I am . . . and Miss says I am'. Long may Caroline and her friends be taken seriously as readers and writers, and listened to in ways we are in danger of losing.

Would the voices of Nathalie and Helen, Caroline and Rebecca be heard in the Gustave Tuck Theatre? Would these girls recognise themselves and their experiences in all the talk of 'pupils', 'students' and 'collective identity'? Is it possible to clear some space at the lectern in order to admit newcomers, outsiders even? In conclusion, I think so, and although it is proving very difficult to get a hearing on an increasingly crowded platform, we *can* continue to put up our hands, interrupt from the floor and call out in class.

Notes

1. 13, 20 and 27 February, 1991.
2. For recent analysis of assessment, testing and the National Curriculum, see Keith Kimberley's articles, 'Dismantling the TGAT Inheritance', *Teaching London Kids*, 26, and 'The Third Limb. Assessment and the National Curriculum', in *The English Magazine*, 23 (The English and Media Centre, London, 1991). Keith's published work, and his research in this area, have consistently examined assumptions behind national testing.Along with others, he has argued hard for curriculum–led assessment and for maximum teacher involvement.
3. Kazuo Ishiguro, *The Remains of the Day*, pp. 28–9.
4. Philip Larkin, *MCMXIV*, in *The Whitsun Weddings*.
5. The phrase comes from James Donald's article, 'Beyond our Ken: English, Englishness, and the National Curriculum', in *Dialogue and Difference. English into the Nineties*, edited by Peter Brooker and Peter Humm,p. 14.
6. See Deborah Cameron and Jill Bourne's paper, *Grammar, Nation and Citizenship: Kingman in Linguistic and Historical Perspective*, Occasional Paper No.1, (Department of English and Media Studies, Institute of Education, 1989). The authors quote from the Newbolt Report of 1921 and from an essay by one of the Newbolt commissioners, George Sampson, also published in 1921, under the title, *English for the English*. Cameron and Bourne's paper was written in response to the Kingman Report but there is much here which pertains to 'Cox'.
7. The Cox Report (7.4)

8. James Donald, op.cit. p. 23.
9. For an account of the origins of this new examination paper, see Peter Traves, 'A Better A Level', in *Eccentric Propositions. Essays on Literature and the Curriculum*, edited by Jane Miller.
10. The word is derived from the seventeenth century French, *marron*, itself a corruption of the Spanish, *cimarron*, which means wild, untamed. It does indeed, as Nathalie said, refer to a class of fugitive slaves living in the mountains and forests of the West Indies. It can refer to a person who is marooned, or, as a verb, to the act of putting a person ashore and leaving him, as a punishment. The word began to be used in the Southern USA to mean camping out for several days, to get away by choice, and this is interesting in the context of Nathalie's suggestion. In any case, the word is linked to a long history of colonization and oppression, and discussion of this resulted from Nathalie's challenge.
11. Jane Miller, *Seductions*, pp. 126-7.
12. James Donald, op.cit. p. 23.
13. Tony Burgess and John Hardcastle, 'A Tale of Three Learners. The Cultural Dimension of Classroom Language Learning', in *Teaching the Humanities*, edited by Peter Gordon.
14. This expression comes from Tony Burgess' essay, 'The Question of English', in *Changing English. Essays for Harold Rosen*, edited by Margaret Meek and Jane Miller, p. 3.
15. 6 March 1991.
16. *Times Literary Supplement*, 22 February, 1991, p.11.
17. Colin MacCabe, 'Language, literature, identity: reflections on the Cox Report', *Critical Quarterly*, 32, 4, p. 11.
18. Colin MacCabe, *The Independent on Sunday*, 10 December 1990.
19. *The Independent on Sunday*, 14 April 1991.
20. MacCabe, *Critical Quarterly*, 32, 4, p. 11.
21. Ibid., p. 12.
22. Ibid., p. 12.
23. Ibid., p. 13.
24. Helen Savva, 'Bilingual by Rights', in *Language and Learning*, 5, pp. 17-21.

Chapter Three
Teaching Popular Culture

Chris Richards

Introduction

This is not the place to write an autobiography but there are reasons here for not suppressing entirely the particular educational history out of which this chapter comes; it is, after all, a part of this book's argument that a curriculum should facilitate reflection upon the located meanings and specific practices of classrooms and the cultures which come within them. I have countered anonymity, therefore, with the names of particular places and, sometimes, of people. But, at another level, what I want to address in this chapter is in part composed by a set of abstract, general terms and the relations between them. The question of cultural identities and of their formation in the relation between family and school, a relation overdetermined and complex, is central. In this context, 'class' will stand for the determinations with which I am here most concerned; this is to some extent a tactical choice motivated by my reading of the Cox Report. There the anxious and euphemistic substitution of 'social group' wherever 'class' might seem the word to use, while consistent with its strategy of balancing homogeneity with diversity, effectively refuses to acknowledge, in any fully explicit sense, a complex social relation central to education. Class is crucially at work in teacher-student relations and is therefore all the more seriously neglected through its elision in Cox. Separating questions of culture from class, and relocating them in a carefully measured acceptance of diversity, achieves much politically. It is a discursive strategy which makes critique seem awkward, rudely disruptive of the consensual embrace offered, it seems, to all reasonable people. So, against that, I will proceed to mark out class as one of my priorities here.

I said this is not the place to be autobiographical, which of course is a warning that I am going to make it just that. Up to a point, anyway. In an academic context, to be 'autobiographical' seems to risk trespassing upon a kind of writing which is achieved mainly by women, balancing the personal within the wider social analysis, where otherwise 'scholarly restraint' is expected. This difficulty, for me, compounds that of making a history of my own educational formation inform and underpin the arguments developed later in this chapter. To start by marking out my own uncertain experience of class is necessary nevertheless. Particular histories matter and the social and institutional position from which I write is no accident. It does seem a messy way to begin when I could cleanly map out debates around class, culture and education and not bother with all this work on personal memory. But some of what is most often excluded from school curricula is necessarily recovered by looking into what is almost forgotten.

Separations
I have given this autobiographical strand the title 'separations', like separating cream from milk, and reminiscent perhaps of those starting points for imaginative and creative writing routinely offered in secondary school English classes. For me the word brings into focus a history of separations which is often coincident with my educational experience and about which I will say at least a little.[1] But 'separations' can be stretched to include the process of writing this chapter – it involves forms of disembodiment, of which I am intermittently aware and which inform what I write. Any writing has a silence and impersonality and is, like this page and those that follow, itself a kind of disembodiment, not a voice, not even that trace of a body, but a configuration of propositions and counter-propositions. To work against that tendency, which will dominate as I go on, I will offer two dates, two years – 1963 and 1974 – and sketch in something of what they mean and why I use them as a way of thinking through my own educational formation.

To begin with I want to dwell on the difficulty involved in defining my own class history. This is a problem which perhaps everyone shares but which for everyone also has its own specificity. I do not think that 'class' was a part of the everyday discourses that I encountered in childhood; but the tripartite distinction between high, low and middle brow comes to mind, remembered as words my parents used, half-understood then as having something to do

with the shape of people's heads. If 'culture' had any meaning for
me in the 1950s and early 1960s, it was not 'common' but divided –
and divided between people distinguished culturally through a
discourse shadowed by evolutionary and biological connotations.
Other, more immediate, divisions were embedded within my own
familial scene and did not make easy a singular sense of who I
might be or what I should become. I still do not feel at ease with the
habit of locating myself in the available categories of class: I cannot
simply recover myself as having had either a 'working-class' or
'middle-class' childhood. It has been easier, and emptier, to settle
for being 'lower middle class'. That way separations get forgotten,
the differences collapsed together. One way of thinking about this is
to mark the uncertainties in my memory of the three fathers that I
knew. Some of the complication of class identity turns around these
three, connected and constituted for me through a marriage made
in the aftermath of World War II.

   If I write about my maternal grandfather I find memories
becoming entangled with parody; to write anything that struggles
free of mockery is probably impossible. So it goes. When I knew
him he lived in an industrial terrace, a house seemingly built over,
and drawing its life from, the coal cellar; the zinc bath was down
there, the toilet across the yard. Douglas Road, Sheffield (that was
the 1950s, it's not there anymore): he worked in the steel mills at the
bottom of the road. It was a place that was for me full of raw and
terrifying noise and grim boasts of danger and sudden death, for
those careless enough to get caught out by the white hot steel
slithering from between the rollers. Thus, I had some contact with
and was able to glimpse the life of heavy manual labour which once
anchored the meaning of 'working class'. My paternal grandfather,
on the other hand, lived in a detached house on Roman Road,
Hereford and wore a tie, a waistcoat, and maintained the
meticulous self-regulations of a local government officer throughout his longer and more respectable life.

   My own more immediate father was a similarly regulated, almost
stoical, figure, an 'assistant county librarian', another local government officer, off to work each day in a suit, the seat of the trousers
shiny from riding his bike. It was three and a half miles from our
semi-detached bungalow to the library, judged to be just the right
distance for a daily ride to and from work, every working day for 25
years, from 1952 to 1977. Those three and a half miles mattered; it
was five miles the other way to the nearest city, Hull. I could say it

was rural and I suppose that it was in a way: farms, market gardens and not much else. But it was not pastoral. We lived near the main road, connecting Beverley and Hull, not in the village, a mile down the lane, between the main road and the river. This is a social geography – I grew up with the boys that lived in and belonged to the village and that went to the school a mile or so up the main road, in another village, so called, big enough to have one – Dunswell County Primary School. I think I have got used to thinking of them, since, as 'rural working class'; but if I was with them I was also separate from them. Somehow at school I felt as if I was left alone by the teacher, that I could get on with what I wanted because I would *get on*. Having a respectable bookish father, and being a book worm, secured for me a privileged space which I could fill with words. Who I was at school, and what I was allowed to become, can perhaps be seen in this way as defined through a condensation of class, gender and familial relations in the figure of my father: it mattered whose son I was and where that placed me in relation to the literate culture of the school.

1963 was the year I took the '11 plus' and moved on to grammar school, in Beverley, where my father worked, a town where he would have been known, at least by the men who taught at the grammar school, as a sober, serious and respectable man. Going to grammar school was both gratification and separation. It was a line scored underneath childhood – a separation, a selecting out, of one identity from others and the fixing, confirmation and proof of my distance from many of those with whom I had spent the preceding six years or so of primary school and childhood. All but one of the boys I knew went to a secondary modern in Cottingham, another route in a different direction, and, as I did sometimes encounter them getting off the bus at the end of the lane where I lived, I would be reminded of what had happened and what it meant. I was thereafter a 'grammar school kid', told to 'get down your own end!'. The fixing of the social relation was rendered as a territorial separation. More refined institutional separations followed. From 1964 I was in the A stream which, as our Latin master reminded us in the moods of sustained fury which seemed to be occasioned by no more than a misplaced conjunction, was to be 'the cream of the cream of the East Riding'. Then, to be brief and suppress much, sixth form, university, First Class Hons., MA, 1974.

Between the summer of 1963 and the autumn of 1974, I had had a little more than 11 years of educational segregation, of being positioned, addressed and formed within progressively more exclusive categories. The social range of friendships, of social connection of any kind, had narrowed relentlessly over those years. So it could have gone on for me; there was nothing 'external' stopping me from moving into research and maybe into a university job for the rest of my life. But in November 1974 I was with primary school children again. I worked with them in a small room at the top of an old elementary school building in Leyton – Downsell Junior School. I was close to them there; I saw no more than six or seven at any time. They were sent to me for a few hours each day, taken out of the larger classes to get some help with their writing, their reading. They were all black, working class; some seemed physically impoverished. I was, and went on being, strung out across the disjunction between my own peculiar literary formation and their particular, immediate and intense negotiations of the school and the time they spent within it. If I was close to them there, then I only had to look out of the high windows, to the blocks of flats extending into the distance, to get the measure of my involvement. In the preceding four years I had read, and listened, my way into a version of black American culture and, bearing a 'knowledge' that was sought after, by-passed 'teacher-training', and became a supplementary teacher for black children. Maybe much of what constituted that knowledge was a fantasy about the lives of others, for with the history of separations that education produces, what counts as knowledge sometimes acquires a fantastic character. In moving abruptly from worrying about cultural theory to being around a working class primary school I had to think through what education enables one to become, what the value of such a 'cultured' identity might be, and what otherwise education might be for.

Recontextualising culture

My brief outline of one kind of division and separation within education could be a way into an argument for the National Curriculum, for the achievement of access to, and the provision of, a standard education for all. But of course the National Curriculum is not about material provision. It relates only to schools in the public sector, and in its formulation of a standard, promotes some very particular versions of what counts as desirable knowledge. The question that I have posed myself here takes this form – In what

ways does the National Curriculum address the separations, dis-
locations and divisions of educational experience which I have
outlined and which characterise most people's routes through
education in Britain? To begin to answer this requires some
attention to what has been held in place. The 'literary experience'[2]
stands at the centre of the Cox Report's construction of a culture to
which all are entitled; and 'culture' is, implicitly throughout, that to
which access is given, not what is made in, and the making of,
everyone's everyday lives.[3]

It is not easy to argue here for an understanding of culture which
no longer takes texts, particularly literary ones, to be central.
Writing this text, to be published, and to argue that culture has to
be understood as less centred on books, is a familiar and contradictory task. There are plenty of books which variously celebrate, defend and theorise the lives of people whose central
experience is not of books but rather of work or streets or television
or some combination of those with other everyday things like eating
meals, sex and talking to people. The social relations through which
such writing is produced are almost invariably those of a middle
class élite anxious at its own isolation from a popular culture which
is always other, always somewhere else. Writing gets yet more
implicated in and defined as particular to a middle class and literary
culture which is marginal to the many who have no sense of
connection with, or belonging to, that culture at all. To privilege the
production of written texts above the centrality of other cultural
practices in other people's lives would be consistent with what has
been a lengthy personal investment. It has always been the way to
get on. But if writing is to be retrieved as a cultural practice,
disentangled from, and produced against the grain of, the élite-
popular relation, then its veneration as an object needs to be
contested. Of course much of what constitutes popular culture does
draw upon a wide variety of forms of writing and to simply
counterpose the 'popular' and the 'written' would be a strange
distortion. The case for refusing to centre culture upon the
production of textual objects at all and thus to embrace a much
broader array of social practices, some of which have no tangible
products, has been made within disciplines such as anthropology
and has been advocated by many of the proponents of Cultural
Studies. Most recently, this issue has been explored by Paul Willis,
and others, in their book *Common Culture*.[4] I want to engage with
their argument here because it intervenes in debates around the

relation of youth to institutionalised culture and represents an important, but problematic, alternative to the account of culture in Cox.

Willis refers to 'the realm of living common culture' in terms which go beyond most of what currently constitutes the field addressed by any subject on the school curriculum, including Media Studies. The list of cultural artefacts is massively extended and, more importantly, there is a central emphasis on culture as activity and as styles of behaviour. This is an emphasis which I intend to take up and mark at various points in this chapter but it is also necessary to take some distance from, and to problematise, the broadly celebratory tone of the book. It is a part of Willis' argument that education almost entirely fails to recognise, connect with or engage the informal culture in which young people locate themselves. He suggests that there is a commonality of informal culture to which education is largely irrelevant. This is an important perception but not one which will surprise many teachers. What needs to be addressed in the course of this chapter is the question of what kinds of engagement, and on what terms, education might have with informal culture. Celebration, fascination and romantic fantasy are flawed responses and not ones which most teachers can live with and sustain. In one sense that is a problem for teachers but it is worth thinking through why it is not the same kind of problem for researchers. Researchers go 'into the field' but teachers tend to stay there for years. I will extend this argument somewhat in a note on 'professional identities' below, but here I want to make a more general observation about everyday lives centred around books.

Within middle-class literary culture to risk moving away from an engagement with the reading, and possibly the writing, of books can be a threatening possibility, a cause of some considerable anxiety; if one does stray too far then at least there is the possibility of maintaining or recovering a secured cultural identity by writing a book about what it was like 'out there'. The people who write about popular culture live and work in book lined rooms, secure retreats. Books are safe, and many, like me, locate their security in them: there is a kind of panic involved in getting too far from them, an anxiety at being cut off, unable to get back. The material and social means through which some people are enabled to anchor themselves in books are substantial and restricted. In the security of possessing and reading books, of having the time, the space, the comfort and the education to enable one to do so, lies a power, obscured, but noticed by those excluded, implicit in having secured that space in which to be left alone.

To be able to write and to write for publication suggests much more – the self-affirmation implicit in addressing an audience of anonymous others in a form which fixes private thought as public discourse is, again, considerable. So, when so many are excluded from these forms of power – excluded often just because so much else in their lives exerts a pressure far greater than that of the school, and education is therefore always at the margin, never a central experience to which time and emotion can be committed with any expectation of 'self-transformation' – is it not frivolous to worry about invoking the standards of a middle-class literary culture to which, surely, access should be given? Is there not a risk, in insisting on the validation of non-literary cultures, that we slide into a cultural relativism which ignores the widely divergent degrees of cultural power attached to the literary and the non-literary? These questions imply what is a familiar and still difficult argument. In the Cox Report there is no equivocation:

> Good schools foster positive attitudes towards books and literature, encouraging pupils to become attentive listeners and reflective readers, library members both in and out of school, and book owners. (3.9).

Most teachers, and my father, would agree with this. What matters, however, is to understand why it can be so problematic to promote this position in practice.

Literary culture
First of all, arguments for entry into the 'literary' tend to promote access to a cultural ideal without much regard for the detail of how that access might be achieved socially and materially. There is also a tendency to evade arguments which both interrogate the power of the 'literary' and direct attention to the power of discourses which are not inextricably implicated in such mysteries. The 'literary' tends to be assumed as a stable and permanent form of élite knowledge which will always be there, standing out above those other lesser knowledges.[5] It is as if power in discourse can only be reached by passing through the 'literary' but, if such a view is still powerful, it is also little more than a relic of liberal humanism. The distinction between the 'literary' and the 'non-literary' is itself

sustained by particular discourses, dividing and ranking those things which matter and those which do not. It is here that Eagleton's argument for an end to the 'literary' and for a reconstitution of 'rhetoric' as a discipline has its place: thus to 'decentre' English would open space for rhetoric as the theory and practice of effective discourse.[6] But before attempting to explore what other forms cultural power might take it is necessary to consider on what basis the Cox Report continues to centre culture around 'the literary' in the National Curriculum's account of English.

It is clear that for this document the 'literary' is the point of departure, and return, from which excursions into the riskier cultural territories can be tolerated and sanctioned. The need for 'analysis' is invoked for those going 'out there' beyond the more secure haven of the literature to which 'we' belong. Such a construction of the cultural field needs to be understood as the still dominant version of an aesthetic account of culture as valued objects. The counter-argument I wish to pursue is that 'culture' is never in any sense given for any of those theoretical and political practices which invoke its value. It cannot be secured in any singular way by one dominant discourse but is a focus of contest between discourses, and is constituted differently by those various discourses. Recalling the work of Volosinov,[7] I want to emphasise that 'culture', the word itself, is multiaccentual. Though it has a broad, if not entirely inclusive, currency as a term used to designate 'things of value', and thus has a strong positive valency, it is nevertheless constantly and simultaneously appropriated by a plurality of competing discourses. The fixing of the 'literary' as pre-eminently cultural is one well-known, but sustained and continuing, accent. It is written into the National Curriculum as if unassailable.

There is a more unrestrained enthusiasm for literature in the Cox Report than for any other dimension of English. It is celebrated as having a 'unique relationship to human experience' and as making available a range that is universal: literature is invoked as overarching all other cultural forms. Within such an elevation of the category of the 'literary' itself, English literature retains its centrality and, though this is less marked in the subsequent programmes of study and levels of attainment, other literatures in English are inscribed as constitutive of 'diversity'. But, going further, the report suggests that:

There is, however, no consensus on which works should be chosen

> from the vast riches of written English and given a privileged status
> in the classroom. Formulations of 'literary tradition', 'our literary
> heritage' or lists of 'great works', however influential their propo-
> nents, may change radically during the course of time. It would be
> wrong, therefore, for us to prescribe a list of set texts (7.14).

As such this hardly seems worth arguing with. But of course what is
not made an object of study here is the process of critical privileging
and the broader formation of cultural hierarchies within which such
particular privileging occurs. Furthermore, whereas in earlier
chapters on language, students and teachers are asked to adopt a
kind of cultural relativism, for literature this is suspended in favour
of the judgement that 'works for detailed study must be of sufficient
substance and quality to merit serious consideration' (7.18).

In those chapters on language, the social world is divided
between a large, and dominant, public domain into which there
should be no intrusion of difference, no violation of the regime of
Standard English, and the periphery in which other, failed, dialects
can be acknowledged:

> Standard English is the language of wider communication. . . .
> Pupils should be able to take the roles in which spoken Standard
> English is conventional: radio presenter, interviewer, expert in front
> of lay audience, etc. (4.50).

In that characteristic evasion of class, Standard English is offered,
with a deceptive modesty, as 'the native language of certain social
groups' (4.11) and any sense of an ongoing struggle in and around
the conventional, legitimate discourse is here ruled out, to use a
Cox key word, as 'inappropriate'. But diversity is not denied:

> . . . language in all its diversity can be approached in a non-
> prescriptive, non-judgemental way . . . it is possible to treat
> systematically and objectively an aspect of human life which is often
> the focus of emotive and prejudiced reactions (6.13).

The priority for learners here is to accept a position from which to
observe, to classify, to describe, to hypothesise and explain (6.12).
The position of learners as actors in a linguistic field fundamentally
shaped by class relations is never directly addressed. Language is
'an important aspect of a person's sense of social identity' (6.18),
Cox says, but identities are made in conflicts which cannot be

contained by teaching students to stick with what is 'appropriate', to avoid 'misunderstandings'.

On the one hand, the relativism teachers are invited to adopt in relation to language opens up that dimension of culture to a diversity but simultaneously abandons a sense of position, engagement and advocacy. The politics in culture, particularly here in language, are eliminated in preference for a controlling, classificatory zeal, a concern with the 'richness of diversity' rather than with linguistic, or other cultural, practices as constitutive of people's various everyday lives. Whereas a relativism about language enables a studious curiosity for all that is excluded from the neutrality and homogeneity declared to govern the public domain, on the other hand, close and sustained contact with writing which is less than literary must be precluded. Such sub-literary materials as 'comic, "fun" poetry, or the lyrics of popular music' are to be 'exploited' as 'a way into the appreciation of a wider range of contemporary writing' (7.21). Clearly students are 'at risk' if the centrality of a commitment to the literary is allowed to waver and the implication is that they will succumb 'in the face of more passive forms of entertainment'. It seems that Standard English is assumed to have such an unshakeable security that a kind of relativism is allowed; the 'literary' is a little more worried by popular culture and, in the 'literary' celebration, there is a defensive note.

In this respect the Report keeps alive traces of the Leavisite legacy and, despite its many specific inclusions of the visual media as legitimate objects of study, their place within the hierarchy of cultural objects is with those other materials where there might be a need to be circumspect, and not with the literature which 'enriches' and enables students to 'grow'.

Cultural practices, activities which are common and everyday, matter less in this version of the curriculum than their products, preferably somewhat isolated and removed from their contexts of production and use. The Cox Report does acknowledge that:

> . . . no position is neutral. Any specification of the curriculum will inevitably contain many assumptions and it would be helpful to make some of them explicit, so that they can be more easily examined and reflected upon by teachers, parents and others concerned with the education of our children (2.4).

In so doing the Report identifies a process which, here and in 7.14

cited above, rather than remaining external to the curriculum, should form a central concern internal to it. It is just such processes of cultural contestation which children, not just 'teachers, parents and others', should be encouraged to explore and understand.

It is the structures and processes of struggles around culture which should inform the development of a more common curriculum rather than any one strategy to secure a new, different or hitherto marginal practice as worthy of cultural status. Of course, historically, the advocacy of film, of television and of the broader range of media has constituted an important phase of upheaval and debate around the relative cultural status of competing cultural objects. But this has tended to be characterised by the serial achievement of a tenuous legitimacy for each successive contender in the struggle for secure space in the curriculum. Now, to privilege any one medium has begun to seem irrelevant to the reality of their social use in complexly inter-related practices – this is both a consequence of broad economic changes in the media and cultural industries and of the patterns of constructive consumption evident in the reception of their products. Selecting out television or film, or popular music, and centring new curricular developments on such single media, while obscuring the actual density of productive relations across the media, must seem curiously blinkered to those whose experience and use of the media involves integrating them into the social routines of the everyday. For most people, what 'the media' are, and what is made of them, cannot be contained by the formal, classificatory, strategies central to academic life. This emphasis is of course pursued by Willis, amongst others, and it is bound to be troublesome for teachers whose professional identities tend to be centred on something more stable, and more clear cut, than the informal practice of everyday life.

Professional identities

It is at this point that I want to both amplify some aspects of the argument made by Willis and to stress how teachers are positioned very differently from ethnographic researchers. For teachers wishing to engage with popular culture there are questions of 'professional' identity, awkward self-identifications as bearers of knowledge and cultural power, to be addressed. Clearly the expanded sense of culture I am pursuing, in combination with an emphasis upon local, particular and evanescent cultural processes, contrasts strongly with the slow pace and institutional timidity of education. It is relatively easy for academic researchers in Cultural Studies to celebrate and publicise a plethora of rapidly self-transforming cultural phenomena. To write from the position of the observer, with no 'obligation' beyond that required of a reasonably sympathetic outsider, allows everything to be recorded with interest and thus added to the fund of ethnographic knowledge accruing to both the individual and the profession. But teachers are supposed to know already, they are supposed to have knowledge and, without it, they are in trouble. To teach in the field of popular culture is to find the field constantly extending beyond the horizon: the faster you move the more there is of it. Strategies of control, of boundary maintenance, become necessary guarantees of professional credibility. It is no surprise therefore that Media Studies in schools stakes its claim to coherence, and cohesion, on a set of key concepts, elastic enough to ensnare whatever the culture out there sets in motion.

A further difficulty besets teachers here: there is both a legacy of teaching as moral intervention and, in part as a consequence of this, a tendency for teachers to form relationships with their students which involve obligations to 'counsel', advise and sometimes confront. The cultural researcher has none of this and can thus defer moral and ideological judgement for the distanced reflection that accompanies the writing, in another place, another, higher, institution, well separated from the school, the street or the youth club. Teachers do not usually have such analytical disengagement from the cultural practices of those they teach and are less likely therefore to indulge in the theorised enthusiasm for symbolic creativity displayed by Paul Willis. Being closer to these creativities can sometimes involve a disturbing coexistence of cultural curiosity with professional censure.

Willis comments disparagingly on 'popular cultural criticism and armchair semiotics' as 'secondhand vehicles . . . for understanding the lived. Viewing life through the glass of symbolic panels. Slumming in safety!' and, rightly, insists on starting with people, a job which is 'messy and hard to do . . . rarely attempted [by] the "cultural experts" [who] stop in their chairs'.[8] But, again, for teachers the distance criticised here is only exceptionally an option. Suppose, for example, that particular people, students in school, explore their symbolic creativity through the production of racist graffiti and actively mark out their identities in rituals of verbal and physical abuse directed at whatever 'racial others' are available.

And suppose that, as a teacher, the responsibility to understand the meaning of these actions for those students is equalled by a responsibility to those 'racial others' and that such a responsibility entails intervention. This is the kind of everyday dilemma which is a part of the work that teachers do. In Willis' account the affirmative value of symbolic creativity is celebrated to such an extent that conflict and contradiction are pushed to the margin of concern. Of course the priority is to counter the aesthetic élitism of identifying culture and creativity exclusively with art. But to found the argument on an empathetic cultural relativism leaves it vulnerable to those who will, with justification, specify to what ends symbolic creativities do turn. In this respect, 'being a teacher' might provide a more secure position from which to contest 'armchair semiotics' than that derived through ethnography.

A rhetoric of empowerment

To secure a consistent sense of identity and purpose as a teacher is a central and continuing problem, particularly where what is offered is so often resisted. One, flawed, solution involves anchoring the practice of teaching in a notion of 'empowerment'. Across a variety of educational discourses, the notion of empowerment continues to seem a credible rationale for teaching which does not simply acquiesce in or explicitly support forms of social inequality: among the current explanations that teachers might offer of their work is the insistence on a power to which others, particularly those most excluded from it, can be given access. On the whole, teachers need to resort to specifically cultural definitions of the power they claim to make available, and display, in their practice. Though different versions of cultural power are invoked, 'empowerment' could even be tied into the more democratic versions of teaching as the transmission of cultural heritage. It might be tempting to insist on retaining the notion of empowerment, free of 'heritage' ties and against the National Curriculum's 'consensus'. But though there may be some persuasive general reasons for making a commitment to education as empowerment, fundamental questions are neglected in doing so. Many writers, speaking from a distance, do advocate empowerment, Gunther Kress[9] for example:

> I think one needs to make students aware, at the very least, of what the structures of domination are and what kinds of objects they have

produced and what kinds of value these kinds of objects have in
society at large.

Kress distinguishes between two kinds of power, 'the power of the
powerful' and 'the power of groups and of individuals in groups not
to conform to the expectations that are generated by the structures
that the powerful have set up'. Education is seen then as a means to
enhance the power of those who do not share in 'the power of the
powerful'. What is neglected here, and by others, is the particularity
of the social relations which compose the contexts of teaching in
that majority of state comprehensive schools where, predomi-
nantly, working class students perceive themselves as being
schooled by middle class teachers. Given such contexts and the
numerous disjunctions which arise there, 'empowerment' appears
an entirely unconvincing rhetorical strategy.

To some extent, the attraction of a rhetoric of empowerment may
well lie in its value as an assertion of a radical professional purpose,
and identity, for those teachers whose experience is of the
immediate futility, and more enduring failures, of schooling. In a
period marked by the erosion of teachers' social status, by relatively
low pay levels and by the increasingly directive central control of
government, it 'makes sense' for teachers more generally to locate
their power in the relation between teachers and students. This is
the 'primary' or definitive relation for teachers and tends therefore
to carry the burden of anxiety over the outcome of all that teachers
do. However, there is something facile about a model of teaching
which implies that with the knowledge passed from teacher to
student, if passed it is, comes power. If that had more than a
rhetorical value, those supposedly less powerful working-class
students would not display such persistent resistance and indifference to the knowledge they are offered.

There are two problems worth addressing here and both need to
be understood as requiring located empirical study if their complexities are to be grasped. These particular problems are constituted
for me through experience as a teacher in London comprehensive
schools and through the experience of working with teachers in the
initial phases of their training. It is important to stress the
institutional position from which these difficulties are defined for I
suspect that they would be construed differently by a researcher
with no personal investment in being a teacher, and therefore
somewhat outside the continual process of self-scrutiny which can

sometimes overwhelm those entering an embattled profession. It is perhaps symptomatic that talk of empowerment is likely to give way to apologies for what, in reality, the particular teacher feels s/he achieves.

First of all, teachers are not perceived by working-class students as powerful people and to equate educational achievement with being able 'to become a teacher' is likely to devalue any such achievement. Secondly, there is little evidence that the cultural power which teachers might see as located in their knowledge is visibly realised in the actual and immediate social relations of classrooms, schools and colleges. I want to develop the first aspect here and resume the second below. To some extent, the 'devaluation of educational achievement' can be understood as evidence of the attack upon education during the last 15 years or so. Educational qualifications retain their value, for some, as a means to achieve ends which lie outside education itself; as such, educational qualifications are worth having in so far as they allow an exit from the contexts in which they have to be acquired. To suggest to working-class students that working hard will get them where 'you' (as teacher) have got is to imply a perpetual return to the place they are often busy trying hard not to be at all. So something other than the assumption that we as teachers have achieved a cultural power which our students will desire is necessary here.

In one inner-London comprehensive school in Pimlico, I once got into a conversation with a 13-year-old boy about educational qualifications. He wanted to know what my qualifications were and, in answering, I began with those which were within the range of compulsory schooling and therefore close to his experience. I could not remember exactly but I said that I had passed perhaps nine or ten GCE 'O' levels. His response was a mixture of amazement and quite conciliatory but excited advice to the effect that I could 'get into computers'. It may be that in part his response was motivated by an awareness that teachers tend to endure relatively low pay levels and that he saw such qualifications as better cashed elsewhere. But I think that he was also surprised that being educationally successful could lead to being a teacher.

In other schools, with a more exclusively working-class composition, I have heard similar, but more antagonistic, expressions of surprise that teachers have degrees and have therefore done well, in a place which such students perceive to be largely closed to them. There is evidence in this of their understanding of the divisions of social territory: the fact that teachers can be successful in middle-class places like universities, to which they have no apparent access, leads to some perplexity over their subsequent presence in a working-class school. Their hatred of school is sometimes hard, as a teacher, to acknowledge. Here is a comment from Archway School in Upper Holloway, London; it comes out of *The Autobiographie of William Heffernan*:

> My life so far has been a waste. The school I am at now must be the worst in London everybody does what they want not many teachers have control over pupils . . . So really this school is a waste . . .
> . . . coming to this school is sheer hell its such a dump it makes you think god not that school again the more you stay away the more you don't want to come back Its a night mare . . .
> The education system in this school needs to be changed yet I can't contribute any idea I would have to sit down and think

He writes of leaving school and going away to Ireland at the end of July 1983. I do not know if he did or not but the wish is of course a common one for working-class students in their last years at school, at the age of 14, 15 or, if they are still there, 16. It is not then so difficult to understand the logic of their sometimes bewildered realisation that teachers have not returned to school because they failed. And as their enquiries tend to culminate with the question – 'So why are you here?' – it might be perceived as mystical to reply – 'I am here to empower you'.

To some extent it is possible to situate this perception of teachers in the context established by Conservative Party strategies to undermine the credibility of teachers and in the not unrelated contempt for teachers demonstrated in much of the press ever since the latter part of the 1970s. But working-class perceptions are not therefore simply versions of a dominant ideology, not the dummy speaking only for the ventriloquist, but are perhaps founded in a more fundamental distance from teaching, if not from teachers. There is a sense in which teaching can appear culturally unattractive: it appears to involve submission to a highly regulated way of life and to a formalised exclusion from popular, informal culture. At Archway School, again, I remember presenting the basis of a critique of *The Sun* to some 15-year-old boys. The context was that newspaper's representation of the so-called 'riots' of the early 1980s. What came out of this for me was the curiously concerned way in which one boy, Brian Murphy, attempted to reassure me that I really should not believe everything I read in the newspapers, 'Don't worry, sir'. It was as if he saw me as suffering a kind of professional anguish in relation to the popular material which he had no difficulty in dismissing as something of a fantasy, a mixture of lies, jokes and games.

So to be the kind of media teacher who conceives the aim of introducing the subject to be that of saving working-class students from subjection to the manipulative products of the capitalist culture industry may lead to some sympathetic challenges to one's misplaced assumptions. The pessimism and cultural despair which has often informed the development of Media Studies should perhaps be countered by a recognition of the elements of 'good sense' specified in the account of popular common sense given by Gramsci:

> ... the healthy nucleus that exists in 'common sense', the part of it which can be called 'good sense' and which deserves to be made more unitary and coherent.[10]

The uneven, multivalent character of common sense suggests that it is to be engaged and debated, not effaced or marginalised or otherwise regarded as an inability to see the power of the media. In a way it is possible to see the boy's response as evidence of an informal appropriation of a mass cultural product which would clearly elude the model of manipulative text and passive recipient which informs the distinction between the 'good' literature and the 'dubious' media. Traces of this are of course apparent in the Cox Report and tend to overshadow the achievement of securing media education within the National Curriculum.

There is in the Cox Report an explicit commitment to the model of teacher-student relations which assumes that the teacher can be a bearer of the knowledge and culture to which the student will aspire. The implication is that the student wishes to become like the teacher, to progress to occupy the position of knowledge which the teacher displays in her or his practice. This conception is proposed with reference to the traditional craft model of learning, the 'apprenticeship', which is perhaps a nostalgic allusion to supposedly more 'authentic' work relations:

> An 'apprenticeship' approach to acquiring written and oral language,

in which the adult represents the 'success' the child seeks and yet offers endless help (3.1).

This is flawed by the assumption of a common class membership between teacher and student. The actual disjunction between classes in schools with many working-class students makes the relation posited here seem utterly improbable. Moreover, to assume that teaching popular culture, or the media, necessarily establishes some commonality is complicated by the fundamentally divergent relations to such culture which often prevail. It may be a matter of a clash between cultural pessimism and gleeful mockery as already suggested in the case of *The Sun*, but it can also be a matter of art house cinema engaging the teacher in contrast with the students' continuing commitment to Australian soap operas. But even where cultural objects are in some sense shared there is an awkwardness about the relation between formal school knowledge and the informal, fluid and expansive everyday intermingling of popular discourses. Media teaching cannot of course bracket out the social relations within which teachers and students encounter each other but, unfortunately it is sometimes assumed that moving away from literary culture achieves exactly that.

I now want to pick up the second difficulty that I marked out in relation to 'teachers' power'. Such power, located in knowledge by the rhetoric of empowerment, is more probably identified by students as inherent in class and institutional position. The power that teachers have in schools and colleges, rather than being perceived as emanating from their formal knowledge, is perhaps seen as separate from such knowledge and as unavailable to students as they are currently positioned in educational institutions. Furthermore, the knowledge (power) which teachers make available may well seem remote from the informal contexts in which students are likely to experience themselves as empowered. It is only through a radical opening of the notion of culture that teachers might be enabled to connect with the sense of cultural agency which their students may experience. One dimension of agency can become apparent within schools when the students act in a crisis to defend their cultural and physical space from the incursions of, for example, the police. This example may be seen as extreme, and certainly it is exceptional, but other, and perhaps more sustained, instances can be documented.[11]

There is a long history of working-class mistrust of the police and, in inner London, black students have had a more than traditional experience of the basis of that mistrust. At Archway School, very early in the 1980s, an incident involving the pursuit and arrest of two students on school premises became the occasion of a serious challenge to the prevailing relations of power between teachers and students. The impetus for such a challenge was carried by a group of black girls in their final year at school and therefore aged either 15 or 16. The school was located very much within a working-class housing estate and was seen by those who attended it as physically a part of their territory, into which teachers came from elsewhere, leaving, of course, to return home at the end of each day. The right of teachers to have control in that physical space was always more precarious than in those schools where there is less of a disjunction between students' and teachers' perceptions. It was suggested that, at the very least, the teachers had declined to intervene with the police, on the behalf of the two students being arrested. It was suspected perhaps that some teachers welcomed the powerful 'reinforcements' which the police provided. The group of black girls insisted on a meeting with teachers and, in that context, insisted that all those present define their relation to the police. Some declared that they felt reassured that the police could be called to the school in the event of trouble – there was much debate about the nature and source of the trouble thus invoked. What the girls wanted, however, was to hear teachers disassociate themselves from the police, acknowledge the racist character of their actions and voice some alliance with the students at the school. This may seem to have little to do with culture and the curriculum but, for them, it involved a heightened sense of cultural agency directed towards securing some degree of negotiated space in a context where middle-class, and mainly white, adults had formal authority. In taking rhetorical action to contest such formal authority the girls constituted themselves as a group with power in a context where it was routinely denied to them.

How agency can be supported through the more usual routines of schools remains problematic. Where protests and dissatisfaction arise over the particular contents, or exclusions, of the curriculum it is essential to connect what might appear to be merely matters of personal taste or idiosyncracy with more explicit understanding of the social relations which underpin such expressions. In this respect, the acknowledgement of 'good sense', implied in taking the variety of grumbles, complaints and silences seriously, also entails reflection upon the middle-class forms of common sense shared by teachers. Such reflection should not be confined to staffrooms but ought to inform, and involve, the students whose 'opinions', 'views' and 'ideas' are seen as legitimate objects of critical, pedagogic, attention. There is a need for teachers to bring into focus something of their own formation and their routes into 'becoming teachers'. As with the example of teaching around *The Sun*, given earlier, it is the disjunction between teachers and students in their relation to cultural objects, and cultural practices, which needs to be made the material of explicit dialogue. It is of more value for both students and teachers to recognise the limits and inadequacies of middle class common sense than to become entangled with the cultural arrogance of a pedagogy centred on 'empowerment'. Formal educational knowledge is not exempt from this, as if it could be entirely separated from the particular class formations of common sense, and needs to develop a more 'self-reflexive' habit. I once taught Jane Austen's novel *Mansfield Park* to a small group of students at Archway School and in that context, where a high proportion of the students' families 'originated' in the Caribbean, it became impossible to proceed without 'decentring' the novel to directly address the history of plantation slavery which one common sense would make marginal. The students' distance from the novel was different from my own but at least we shared a mutual 'unease' which both opened up a history otherwise absent from the curriculum and made an explicit discussion of the English Literature syllabus possible and important. Their dissatisfaction, their boredom even, can be read as cultural agency, though apparently contained within a few lessons in one room involving just a handful of people.

Important developments in media education, particularly where emphasis is placed on practical production, do allow a transfer of responsibility to students. Moreover, it is more possible to make the school a place in which to work and in which resources are made available without privileging teachers as sources of power to whom students must defer. Media Studies can provide situations in which students are less likely to experience themselves positioned as needing 'to be empowered' and might thus act to produce what they wish rather than devote so much energy to resisting and resenting the unequal relation in which they feel themselves placed. The frequent unfamiliarity of teachers with the technology and practices of media production is also, again, an occasion for both some reflection on the separation of 'academic' from 'practical' knowledges in the education of teachers and for students to witness their teachers placed as learners, and making mistakes.

There is scope here for going beyond the type of locally articulated challenge I have described above, by moving to engage with forms of discourse which have a currency in the broader public domain. In this respect the authors of *Education Limited*[12] reflect usefully upon the limits of challenge as such:

> It may need a further set of practices – of representation, social recognition, or political organization – to make resistance into more than challenge.

It is useful to recall Eagleton's view of rhetoric here, with his stress on the use of discourse in the public sphere. The field of public discourse, in which media forms are pervasive, can be engaged through placing students as producers of such forms. But such production has to enable them to work on their situated concerns. In the process of representing such concerns in more public forms, they are necessarily reflecting on their existing implicit knowledge of the particular medium and moving into 'forms of *activity* inseparable from the wider social relations between writers and readers' and, perhaps, finding, and developing, 'the most effective ways of pleading, persuading and debating'.[13] The potential of media production in education is considerable, but not guaranteed, and it is important to note the need for more empirical investigation of this practice. The best documented instances here are of video production within formal education and, outside it, of building on popular photographic practices to engage 'students' in explorations of social identity in families, with friends and at work.[14]

It is necessary then to get beyond thinking of culture as objects and of addressing popular culture as a matter of adding in all the objects that lie 'out there'. Culture, popular culture, needs to be understood as practice and as a practice in which a kind of 'self-production' can take place. The extension of the curriculum to include comics, pop videos, soap operas and advertisements rather than novels, poems and short stories is unlikely to provide the commitment to learning which one might expect; often such inclusions are met with indifference or, from middle class students, with doubts of their legitimacy as objects of study. Without contexts in which a sense of agency in engaging with these things can be produced, choices between objects of study make too little difference. Media Studies does allow or produce some sense of debate around what counts as valued knowledge and can facilitate reflection on those cultural objects which have a central place in students' lives. It is essential that such work continue and be expanded. However, Media Studies, with its giving of space to varieties of adolescent and working-class 'taste', can also seem no more than a kind of 'tokenism' and is most often a kind of ceded space where all that might trouble other areas of the curriculum can be *allowed*. The lack of power carried by its knowledge is perhaps illustrated by the limited involvement of middle-class students – at least at the secondary level where Media Studies has a history of absorbing all those working-class students who 'could not' be taught English Literature.

To go beyond the rhetorical advocacy of Media Studies, it has to be located in terms of the broader social relations of the teaching situation where, it seems, teachers inhabit one world and working-class students another and their uncomfortable coexistence in the same building is registered at the level of (in)discipline, truancy, apathy and sometimes a wearying daily antagonism. For a National Curriculum to announce access to a standard, and standards of, knowledge to which all are entitled misses the point entirely. It is the active refusal of what is offered in education which is the most pervasive and intractable difficulty faced by teachers in schools with a largely working-class composition. The general principles of curriculum construction of importance here are these: the meanings, values and specific differentiations of the 'cultural' have to be open to continual contest and negotiation and the social relations of the educational context (which exceed most, if not all, definitions of the cultural) have to be made visibly open to interrogation. 'Empowerment' is otherwise too much a matter of teachers reassuring themselves that they have power and that, at the same time, it can be given to those who have less. If teaching is to enable students to understand their lives, and, if they wish, to change the circumstances in which they live then the power to do so has to be experienced as such within the educational setting itself rather than be deferred constantly or invoked as a kind of abstract potential. The reading of media texts is increasingly understood more as an activity of rhetorical self-definition and less as passive consumption. What people should do with the media is not simply inscribed in media products but is substantially redefined on their terms.

Similarly, being a learner, like being a consumer, can take on the more productive sense of reworking what education makes available in the more fluid, complex and particular terms of those thus positioned. What I am restating here is at least partly a further acknowledgement of the argument pursued by Willis. If people can engage with 'consumer products' and appropriate them into their local and particular informal cultures as, for example, has happened with 'trainers',[15] then there seems to be some basis for approaching education not with old models of passive consumerism in mind but with a rather less patronising set of expectations about what it is that might be made out of the lessons which teachers provide.

Some conclusions
To bring this kind of chapter to a conclusion is always difficult. There is nothing easy about proposing alternatives from within a history beset with failures and frustrations. In thinking around alternatives to the National Curriculum, I have centred on the problems which arise in seeking to offer either access or empowerment to working-class students. Whatever I might suggest here seems doomed to meet all my own objections, to either intention, head on. Even arguments for changing teacher-student relations in secondary schools, relations which turn around a denial of intellectual responsibility to children, will probably founder against the common experience of middle-class students moving in to use and dominate whatever democratic structures, internal to the school, might be established. To attempt to 'enfranchise' students without radically redefining how varieties of non-school knowledge and experience might be valued may do no more than secure existing advantage. This is a problem to which I will return but it may be more productive to approach the issue differently by looking first at how what counts as education for middle-class students might be further problematised and reconstructed. It is here that some of the curiosities of my own autobiographical notes can be worked over as the basis of a broader argument.

I said in my introduction that the question of cultural identities should be central and that I would be concerned with their formation in the relation between family and school. I want to stress again how a particular version of middle-class, grammar school, education works to separate out and secure one kind of identity, and to suppress others. Cultural identities are produced in 'informal' contexts but they are also constituted through a relation to specific forms of work and, in this respect, cultural differences are mapped onto social hierarchies. The National Curriculum's 'Non-Statutory Guidance' notes that 'Pupils should draw on their cultural identity'[16] but, as elsewhere, class is less a referent of the 'cultural' than 'race', ethnicity or religion. Accounts of culture which make class and work integral to identity are not addressed by the National Curriculum and in this it is consistent with the educational experience constructed by the middle-class school recalled in my autobiographical introduction.

At school, I am sure that I never had occasion to write anything at all about work, places of work or the people that worked in them. The boundary between what counted as appropriate knowledge, experience and discourse in school and what might take hold of emergent selves outside was, and is, both remarkably firm, and for those regulated by it, elusive. The three fathers that I conjured out of memory came into this piece of writing in terms of the houses in which they lived and the work that they did: these male identities anchored thus never came within the range of any lesson. The work of the working class, steel production in Sheffield for example, probably occupied no more than an insignificant paragraph in some Geography homework, written, revised, forgotten. It was consistent with middle-class identity for work to be kept out of education, to be made remote. Whatever I might have known of the conditions of work, the anxiety, and male bravado, of working in a steel mill must have remained personal, unspoken and unexamined. The 'culture of the work-place' could hardly be expected in a 1960s grammar school curriculum but it is still not, in any adequate sense, a part of education in British schools.

The exclusion of a wide array of forms of work from the production of educated adult selves persists. The formation of a middle-class literary person involves an investment which becomes self-regulating. No trace of summer jobs labouring in a Brighton brewery or on construction sites in Florida ever impinged upon the essays that I wrote, even if they were about 'industrial' novels, alienation, or racial divisions in the southern States. Successful academic writing was defined, though nobody said so exactly, by its demarcation from modes of writing which rework the personal experience of the writer. Summer jobs, however disturbing, were just transient experiences and never allowed to sever the spine of a bookish identity. In St Petersburg, Florida, where I worked at/got fired from various jobs, I joined the local library and spent evenings struggling to read after a day of pick-axe work in high humidity. I had to keep reminding myself who and what kind of person I was.

Classrooms were the first places of work which I ever had to write about. They had to be faced and lived with for longer than anywhere else I had ever worked and the people I worked for wanted me to document what I did and why. At the top of Downsell Junior School, late in 1974: writing a brief document of the few months I spent there opened up a continuing attempt to do something which engaged with a personally immediate experience but in terms that pointed towards a more systematic, cultural, understanding.

There are two substantive points to draw out more explicitly here. There is an argument for what I have called 'depersonalisation' and, also, a different kind of argument about identity and work. First, my argument against the separation of formal educational knowledge from experience which lies beyond its bounds is not an argument for 'personal writing' but is orientated towards a process of 'depersonalisation':

> In *teaching* the general strategy should be to render the personal impersonal, to address and to redefine what is constitutive of the personal in terms which invite examination and questioning of those boundaries between what is thought of as the individual, and the social matrix out there.[17]

In using such a term I want to stress the productive relation between formal systems of concepts and personal experience. The emphasis here recalls something of the relation between 'common/good sense' and formal education in Gramsci's terms but also connects with the work of Vygotsky, and in particular his examination of the relation between 'spontaneous' concepts, which seem to derive more from informal cultural contexts, and the more formal, systematic, or 'scientific' concepts which education makes available. The importance of Vygotsky is that, perhaps more than Gramsci, he does emphasise a developmental relation between these different orders of knowledge rather than a displacement of what has been learnt before education is able to intervene.

The case for attending to forms of work derives its momentum from the critique of middle-class education which has emerged from my autobiographical reflections. The connection between the argument for 'depersonalisation' and the concern with work, and the cultures it sustains, is made in the refusal of work as an experience to be either assimilated to personal writing or excluded as antithetical to the proper concerns of education. Places of work are important, and different, sites of experience for middle-class and working-class students and such places should be made objects of study. By working on, rather than excluding, such a central basis of cultural division it becomes a little more possible to conceive of a common curriculum in which difference is addressed rather than managed.

In the most general terms my argument has been for a curriculum which gives a central place to the understanding of the social relationships within which cultural knowledge is produced and variously valued, restricted or shared. And such an emphasis necessarily turns back upon the curriculum itself, giving ground to questions like – What is this for? Why are we doing this? How is this going to help us? Towards the end of the compulsory phase of schooling these questions get asked again and again, by people no longer willing to be kids, too big to be pupils, and most often by those whose relation to education has not been one of comfortable acquiescence but is fractured by doubt and uncertainty. Perhaps it is hard for teachers not to be impatient with such questions when their lives are centred both within the obviousness that pervades the value of learning and a self-protective disdain for much of what counts as work 'out there'. 'Work experience' schemes have sometimes been resisted as invasive strategies designed to take the learning out of education and replace it with vacuous instruction in the routines of labour. This is a justified resistance where such schemes seem no more than a means to shuffle off the working-class students the school no longer wants. But if the experience of work was made an integral concern for all those involved in education, and made the object of a more investigative and critically ethnographic initiative then there would be scope to secure a socially self-reflexive education and thus a context in which questions asked by awkward students would have a central place.

In a context where both the production of a scholarly élite, 'the cream of the cream', and the training of a subservient work-force, had been refused, it might well be more possible to establish a sense of cultural agency within schools and as an everyday fact rather than an outcome of the extraordinary, crisis, moments recalled earlier. The authors of *Education Limited* advocate a similar linkage of curriculum and questions of power in their emphasis on 'an ongoing discussion of social objectives and cultural differences, right up to the modification of forms of social power within the institution itself'. But they also acknowledge that:

> On their own, schools can never remove inequalities; what they can do is to provide a sphere in which they are revealed and contested, and therefore some of the conditions, especially some subjective ones, for their removal.[18]

In this they avoid what I have called the 'rhetoric of empowerment' and the fantasy of intervening to dissolve broader sets of social relations.

The argument pursued by Paul Willis shifts attention from work as a site of cultural activity and self-production. It is argued that informal culture, defined largely through its association with 'leisure' rather than school or work, involves and has the everyday emotional investment of youth in general and that, however diversified such cultures might be, there is nevertheless something 'common' about them. Willis offers two principal meanings for 'common': 'everywhere, resistant, hardy' and 'shared, having things in common'. If commonality of some kind is produced through involvement in such informal, 'common' culture, are the divisions which education in Britain insists upon largely subverted by all that educational institutions, however powerful, cannot touch? Willis argues that:

> . . . elite or 'official' culture has lost its dominance. It has certainly always been honeycombed with subterranean resistances and alternatives but now the very sense, or pretence, of a national 'whole culture' and of hierarchies of values, activities and places within it is breaking down.[19]

Given this perspective, it is not surprising that education hardly forms a central component in the arguments, and proposals, which he and his fellow researchers develop. 'Education' is given a breadth and informality which takes it out of the hands of teachers and other professional educationalists:

> Making (not receiving) messages and meanings in your own context

and from materials you have appropriated is, in essence, a form of education in the broadest sense. It is the specifically developmental part of symbolic work and creativity, an education about the 'self' and its relation to the world and to others in it. Where everyday symbolic work differs from what is normally thought of as 'education' is that it 'culturally produces' from its own chosen symbolic resources.[20]

In this view, education as presently constituted, or reconstituted with the National Curriculum, has no more than a slight connection with the lives of most of those who 'pass through' it. Again, Willis comments:

The field of education is likely to come under even more intense pressure. It will be further marginalized in most people's experience by common culture. In so far as educational practices are still predicated on traditional liberal humanist lines and on the assumed superiority of high art, they will become almost totally irrelevant to the real energies and interests of most young people and no part of their identity formation. Common culture will, increasingly, undertake, in its own ways, the roles that education has vacated.[21]

Willis is right, but right from a distance: he shares too much in the subjective marginalisation of education by working-class youth. Education does of course contain within it the elements Willis contests and these continue to be an unbroken thread in the formation of middle-class identities. In this respect, education does still play its part in securing the advantage of those who already have access to a broader social power. The difference between being 'irrelevant' to most, and being 'irrelevant' to all, young people is marked by class. Education has its part in producing social divisions afresh and to attribute a superior potency to the sphere of informal culture, though confirming the particular perceptions of those he celebrates, seems no more than an act of tactical optimism. The wider social relations within which cultural creativity has its life are not, as Willis himself argued in *Learning to Labour*,[22] necessarily transformed by strategies of symbolic resistance. To some extent too it is likely that education does still succeed in producing subjects who believe in and thus bear the responsibility for their own failure. Schools still mark working class identities, and the marks tend not to be good.

But Willis is also wrong about education. English and Media

Studies in schools are not so bounded by established cultural hierarchies as his more dismissive general observations imply. Much of what has developed in the last 10 or 15 years has struggled to address the disjunction between informal culture and the school curriculum and, though too little of it is written into the National Curriculum, that practical knowledge survives and continues to expand among teachers of those subjects. Nevertheless, his stress on the fluidity and breadth of culture underlines the need to make formal concepts something other than a net in which to entrap popular culture. Concepts, and the vantage points to which they may give access, should allow students to think through their own positions and enable them 'to think beyond their means'.[23] As I have suggested, similar formulations can be found in Gramsci's work[24] and in that of Vygotsky[25]. Here I want to insist on a need to make more of opportunities to historicise, to unravel the surfaces of the contemporary. There is a need to teach popular culture through forms of investigative study which provide conceptual means for purposes defined by students themselves. Popular culture has a popular history in which students are themselves participants, inheriting, reworking and interrogating past formations. It might then be possible to work through generational transitions in popular culture and the histories of people's self-constructions in earlier formations. Willis refers to teenage and early adult experience as formative for the rest of their lives – so how have those thus placed in earlier moments reworked those early affiliations as they moved through youth into adult lives? It is here too that familial relations and family histories become central and such situated learning can connect with wider debates around gender and class and, indeed, race.

One purpose of the autobiographical elements in this essay has been to open up a 'dialogue' with readers: it was in part a way of bringing into play readers' own reflections on their education and what kind of identities it seemed 'set up' to produce. I have attempted to read educational policy in terms of the cultural identities it prefers and, in its implementation, seeks to produce. Placing my emphasis on how elements of past educational separations are perpetuated in current policy and how such divisions might be interrogated in a more common curriculum illuminates the limits of the National Curriculum's account of culture and, I hope, directs attention to a different set of priorities.

If you are still wondering what Paul Willis and Brian Cox are

doing here together in the same article, when they are clearly
writing across irreconcilable distances, I will at least try to be
straight about it. For me, there is a strong temptation to go along
with the aspect of Willis which argues that education has little
future as an institution for young people, for those who attend
under compulsion. That kind of account connects with too much of
my experience of teaching to be dismissed easily. His argument is
problematic nevertheless; I have attempted to show why but also to
do something with it. Cox is oddly seductive. It is another kind of
temptation. I can see why many teachers will feel that they can
settle for this, that it is an acceptable account of what English and
Media teaching should be. So back to Willis to remind myself that
culture is not contained by the consensus Cox appears to construct.
Cultural activity exceeds and defies the central concerns of the Cox
Report. He indulges a retrospective and selective engagement with
some challenges to traditionalism but seems unaware that other
kinds of questions are posed everyday in classrooms where the most
fundamental assumptions about what education might be for get
turned over and thrown back at those that hold them. There are
other ways of thinking about that kind of challenge which do not
come within the progressivism Cox claims to have assimilated.
None of these conclusions conclude anything; they mark points of
transition and difficulty and, at best, reopen an argument that
might otherwise seem closed.

Notes
One part of this chapter, 'A Rhetoric of Empowerment', was presented to a
'Media, Culture and Curriculum' symposium at the Annual Meeting of the
American Educational Research Association, Chicago, April 3–7 1991.

1. It was Keith Kimberley who suggested, several years ago, that I write
   up something of this educational history. Unfortunately Keith died, in
   January 1991, as I was completing the first draft of this chapter. I also
   want to acknowledge many apposite conversations, at various times,
   with Elizabeth Rouse, Dr K. Ghaffari and Joyce Little.
2. The Cox Report, Chapter 7: Literature paragraphs 7.1, 7.3 and 7.5
   suggest the more extensive privileging of the literary experience.
3. The Cox Report assumes that the central issue to be addressed is that
   of access to a culture which can only be recognised in its institutional
   legitimation. Or, as the Beverley Grammar School motto had it:
   '*Adolescentiam Alunt Senectutem Oblectant*' – 'They nurture the
   young and are the solace of old age' (books, of course).

4. Paul Willis (with Simon Jones, Joyce Canaan and Geoff Hurd), *Common Culture: Symbolic work at play in the everyday cultures of the young*, Open University Press, Milton Keynes, 1990.

5. In the words of the Kingman Report: 'Wide reading, and as great an experience as possible of the best imaginative literature, are essential to the full development of an ear for language, and to a full knowledge of the range of possible patterns of thought and feeling made accessible by the power and range of language' (7.2).

6. Terry Eagleton, 'The End of Criticism', in *English in Education*, Summer 1982, 16, 2; and Terry Eagleton, *Literary Theory An Introduction*, Basil Blackwell, Oxford, 1983.

7. V. N. Volosinov, *Marxism and the Philosophy of Language*, translated by Ladislav Matejka and I. R. Titunik, Seminar Press, New York, 1973.

8. Willis, op. cit., p. 6.

9. 'Two Kinds of Power: Gunther Kress on Genre', an interview, *The English Magazine*, Nr 24, The English and Media Centre, London, 1991.

10. Antonio Gramsci, *Selections from the Prison Notebooks*, edited and translated by Quintin Hoare and Geoffrey Nowell Smith, International Publishers, New York, 1973, p. 328.

11. A brief chronology of broader protests in which school students have involved themselves is worth recording here: 1976–1980: participation in protests against ILEA's programme of secondary school closures and amalgamations; 1979: protests against the effects of teachers' 'industrial action' (the closing of schools at lunchtimes); 1981–8: participation in protests against successive proposals to abolish ILEA; 1984/5: action in Newham and Tower Hamlets against racist attacks; 1986: walkouts in support of Militant-organised strike against YTS; 1985–7: sporadic support for teachers' industrial action over pay and conditions; 1991: Hornsey. Walkout against British support for Gulf War.

12. Cultural Studies (various authors), *Education Limited*, Unwin/Hyman, London, 1991.

13. Terry Eagleton, *Literary Theory*, pp.205–6.

14. See the following: Roy Stafford, 'Redefining Creativity: Extended Project Work in GCSE Media Studies' and Jenny Grahame, '*Playtime*: Learning about Media Institutions through Practical Work', both in David Buckingham (ed.) *Watching Media Learning: Making Sense of Media Education*, Falmer Press, London, 1990: Andrew Dewdney and Martin Lister, *Youth, Culture and Photography*, Macmillan, London, 1988 and Philip Cohen, *Really Useful Knowledge: Photography and Cultural Studies in The Transition*

From School, Trentham Books, 1990; and, also of interest, Jo Spence, *Putting Myself in the Picture*, Camden Press, London, 1986.

15. See Daniel Miller, *Material Culture and Mass Consumption*, Blackwell, Oxford, 1987 and the work of David Morley and Roger Silverstone at the Centre for Research into Innovation, Culture and Technology at Brunel University. Perhaps also see Spike Lee's 'Do the Right Thing', Universal, 1989, for Nike Air Jordans and much else besides.

16. See *English in the National Curriculum*, No. 2, and the *English Non-Statutory Guidance*.

17. Chris Richards, 'Anti-Racist Initiatives', *Screen*, Volume 27, Number 5, September–October 1986, p.77. An account of the gendered negotiation of Media Studies is contained in my 'Intervening in Popular Pleasures: Media Studies and the Politics of Subjectivity', in D. Buckingham (ed.) *Watching Media Learning: Making Sense of Media Education*, Falmer Press, London, 1990.

18. *Education Limited*, p. 40.

19. Willis, op. cit. p. 41.

20. Ibid., p. 42.

21. Ibid., p. 147

22. Paul E. Willis, *Learning to Labour: How Working Class Kids get Working Class Jobs*, Saxon House, Farnborough, 1977. It is a familiar criticism of Paul Willis' work that he centres too exclusively upon 'male experience'. This emphasis is also apparent in my reports of classroom encounters. It may be that the relation of working-class girls to education and to teachers is inadequately represented here. Such differences are a matter for further empirical research.

23. James Donald, 'On the Threshold: Psychoanalysis and Cultural Studies' in *Psychoanalysis and Cultural Theory: Thresholds*, edited by James Donald, Macmillan, London, 1991.

24. Gramsci, op. cit.

25. L. S. Vygotsky, *Thought and Language*, edited and translated by Eugenia Haufmann and Gertrude Vakar, MIT, Cambridge, Mass., 1962; L. S. Vygotsky, *Mind in Society: The Development of Higher Psychological Processes*, edited by Michael Cole *et al.*, Harvard University Press, Cambridge, Mass., 1978. Also, see David Buckingham's editorial contributions to *Watching Media Learning*.

Chapter Four
The Multicultural Politics of Teaching English

Robert Owens

'Something needs to be done'

It has not been uncommon, of late, for concerns about education, about cultural differences, and about the British manifestations of the 'Rushdie Affair' as inflamed 'effects' of those differences, to tumble together in anxious forebodings about 'our' national culture, and the lack of consensus within it. Members of the Cox Committee, architects, practically, of the National Curriculum in English, were alarmed and motivated by what Professor Cox has described as the 'tension' between national unity and cultural diversity, a tension enacted by Muslims in Bradford taking to the streets.[1] Members of the liberal-left establishment are no less anxious about the nation in smithereens: 'Our attempt at multi-culturalism has failed', writes Fay Weldon, 'The Rushdie Affair demonstrates it'.[2]

This chapter is about the multicultural politics of teaching English, in the light of the Cox Report and the National Curriculum in English. It is also about the hegemonic 'logic' of the 'new' English, the cultural hospitality that it has enjoyed. To these ends, selected cultural data accumulate as the chapter progresses, principally: the Cox Report; the Rushdie Affair; the altered reputation of British Muslims; Fay Weldon's 'CounterBlast' *Sacred Cows*; formulations of 'multiculturalism' and 'postmodernism'; putative crises of identity (individual and national); and the cultural 'revival' of 'Literature'.

'Us' and 'Them'

National identity is a hegemonic expedience. It serves the interests of those groups that manage to define 'the nation' in their own image. It is an imperative of the New Right: '. . . the state of nationhood is the true state of man,' wrote John Casey in the *Salisbury Review*, 'and danger of ignoring the sentiments of nationhood is actually the danger of the destruction of man as a political animal'.[3] National identity struggles to become more pressing in people's lives than other cultural affiliations. Stalwarts of national identity favour the formula 'Us' and 'Them', that 'violent hierarchy',[4] whose seminal Christian metaphor is God and the Devil, good and evil. Feisty Argies and pre-Glasnost Soviets made good devils, good musterers of 'Us', in their day. But Europeans – white, capitalist and democratic, too much like 'Us' – have not. The proposition that full membership of Europe might contaminate 'our' national character – Jean-Marie le Pen shares Mrs Thatcher's fear of what he has called the 'Brussels virus'[5] – failed, in Britain, to whip up sufficient Europhobia to win for itself hegemonic plausibility.

It is white, Christian Europe that is phobic. Its latest 'Them' is the putative rise of Islamic fundamentalism, which, it is feared, has begun to infect the cultural integrities of some of its nation states.

M. le Pen, who ranks the 'problem' of Islam as one item on a shopping list of other 'Thems' – 'terrorism, gangsters, drug traffickers and financial crime' – views the 'rise of Islam' and 'immigration from outside Europe' as one problem.[6] As a result of the Rushdie Affair, he finds himself in rather more 'liberal' company than he is accustomed to. This is Anthony Burgess:

> The stupidity of the Islamic deathmongers, burning a book they do not have the intelligence to understand . . . portends a situation that Chesterton foresaw at the beginning of this century – the renewal of an ancient and basic struggle which the distraction of the Cold war temporarily occluded. In other words, we know our enemy.[7]

Know thy enemy: know thyself. The cultural software was always in place in the West to compute Arabs and Asians, for centuries fantastic and fascinating in Western misrepresentations of them, as 'Other', as 'Them'. Lately, 'We' have jeered at their 'philistinism', and scared ourselves with conjurings of mad, murdering mullahs, and ritualistic book burnings.

The Gulf War provided a golden opportunity for parts of the British media to taunt 'our' new demons, to remind the nation about who it needs to either expel or assimilate in order to become itself again, and to point up the 'folly' of multiculturalism in terms that M. le Pen would put his weight behind:

> True Brits everywhere are flying the flag in support of our lads in the Gulf. But in some parts of the country spineless town hall traitors are ordering the Union Jack to be pulled down. Why? Because they are afraid that our national flag may upset the Muslim minority who have chosen to make their homes here, enjoying the benefits of *our* social security, *our* council housing, *our* Health Service. Tough![8]

'Us' and 'Them'. When the nation deploys its troops and pulls itself together, those slumbering contraries return. Some of us *are* Muslim: we *are* in part what 'We' are persuaded to loathe. The nationalist 'We' only countervails by silencing many of the nation's constituent voices. It was not a united nation that took part in the military campaign against *the people* of Iraq. The national 'We' sounds hoarse, ironic, embarrassed.

Snug, smug first person, sly trope of hegemony, this 'We' is all the more insidious for declaring itself liberal and non-racist. It hides its intolerance of cultural difference behind a declared 'colour-blindness': the nation, by all means, may be multi*racial*, but not multi*cultural*. It is a case of 'When in Rome', as benign as that. For 'When in Rome' read 'When at school'. What better place to turn cultures into culture, entrench the national 'We', than in schools where all the nation's young are in the making?

Common sense
Debates about education never go short of participants, some of them worthy and informed. Unfortunately, those who have dominated the current debate always get their say and have the cultural power to get heard. Like shrapnel, their frantic, pernicious slogans have cut and wounded every which way. Among them: falling, or fallen, standards; lazy and incompetent teachers; all ideology, no education; all theory and no practice in teacher-training institutions; flabby, woolly curricula; too much do-good concern with equal opportunities, pandering to ethnic minorities while denying 'our' children the attention that is their cultural right; nothing can be worse than what went before. Sound-bites of that kind, neat and sealed, viral and infectious, catch on fast. They strut like natty conclusions of sensible debate when in fact they are choked up as the first reactions of tangled guts, seized as the

premises that debate might reasonably proceed from, resistant to
the complexities of that which they have already misrepre-
sented.

Yet they bask in common sense. A common sense that has shown
little sign of abating. On the contrary, if Kenneth Baker is to be
believed, it is 'back in fashion'.[9] A National Curriculum makes
common sense. Common sense has had it that all things should be
common, from curricula to culture. 'Common' has been inflected
by the rhetoric of the Right to come to mean 'in everybody's
interests', and, rabidly over-used, has quickly been established as a
colloquialism of National Curriculum sales talk. There is an
impeccable balance to the claim, a seemingly tautological one, that
a common curriculum makes common sense because it fosters a
common culture. Try rocking *that* boat. Like 'standards', common
sense seems anonymous, non-ideological, non-partisan, always-
already consensual. Its wisdoms are to be imbibed acognitively. Its
stowaway is ideology.

Education reform appeared to extend naturally from a paradigm
of consensus whose theme was common sense. Common sense
claimed a monopoly on reason across the political-discursive
spectrum. It got to discursive sites first, cultivated them, set agendas
on them, and proved, by and large, successful at seeing off those
challenges that wanted to attend to the exigencies of *difference* in
cultural life, of what we have *not* got in common.

A paradigm of 'consensus' is nourished by the sheer diversity of
enunciative occasions on which similar views are expressed.
Hegemony thrives on *rendezvous*. If people of different persuasions
say the same thing often enough, it must be right. The Gulf War
was an instance of such a consensus-effect in Britain: right, left and
centre, the House approved it. Or so we were led to believe. Those
front-bench members who dared not to were told to shut up or get
out. That's how 'consensus' works.

To audit the hegemonic process that has marshalled *enough*
consent to the Right's education reform, you need to convene the
scattered, variously motivated voices that have coincided in
genuflection to it. Put differently, 'common sense' is an ideological
hybrid, a cultural mongrel. Hence its vigour. The absorption of the
public debate on education into a paradigm of 'consensus' and
'common sense' is a strategy you would associate with the Right.
But education-policy-as-common-sense has found willing enun-
ciators at the heart of the liberal-left establishment. Such has

been its hegemonic stealth, it has even crept into discourses of 'dissent'. Fay Weldon's *Sacred Cows*, one of Chatto and Windus's 'CounterBlasts', a 'forum for voices of dissent' which 'challenge the dominant values of our time',[10] is a case in point.

Liberal turns

In the name of Freedom of Belief we dwell contentedly (or thought we did) in our multi-cultural, multi-religious society: it doesn't work, but who dares say so?[11]

Fay Weldon dares, and she is by no means alone. As a result of the Rushdie Affair, the view that British Muslims represent the unacceptable excesses of multiculturalism, that something needs to be done about them, has become perfectly orthodox. It makes common sense to think that way. Bitten by 'the painful awareness of common sense',[12] Fay Weldon concludes: 'Our attempt at multiculturalism has failed. The Rushdie Affair demonstrates it'.[13] Like Professor Cox, she argues for a 'common culture', at least in schools, where the impact of the Education Reform Act 'can't be worse than what went before'.[14] 'What went before' includes the multicultural 'idealism' of the 1970s, the 'paralysis of the well-intentioned'.[15] Fay Weldon recalls the Bullock Report of 1975:

No child should be expected to cast off the language and culture of the home as he/she crosses the school threshold, nor to live and act as though school and home represent two totally separate and different cultures'.[16]

Oh yes they should:

Of course there is racism in our schools, amongst our children, each group clinging to its own, disliking the other, if this nonsense is spoken, believed, fought for. The uniculturalist policy of the United States *worked*, welding its new peoples, from every race, every nation, every belief, into a whole: let the child do what it wants at home; here in the school the one flag is saluted, the one God worshipped, the one nation acknowledged. . . . Our children would grow up with a sense of common identity – be they Afro-Caribbean, Asian or European in origin – not paralysed by confusion. Your God or mine? Your curry or my chips? Your sister on the hockey field, my brother down the mosque? No-one prepared to say – or only the Muslim – our God is better than yours.[17]

In *Sacred Cows*, Fay Weldon writes aghast about police racism in Britain, and about the kinds of racism associated with the National Front; she defends the right of a British-Asian author to write about 'the sickening racism of this country of ours, the dreadful indignities, the awful absurdities endured by our immigrant population'; she distances herself from the literary establishment whose 'vague racism' she suspects.[18] Fay Weldon is *no racist*.[19] She is as anti-racist and 'well-intentioned' as we writers, and presumably readers, of this book suppose ourselves to be.

No racial bigot, Fay Weldon might be considered a cultural one. She advocates restricting the access of British Muslims to their own culture, their own identities, and turning them into 'Us'. But only in order to save them from themselves, stop them getting beaten up, complete their membership of the national 'We'. She wants to make British Muslims properly 'human', and properly 'national'. Like 'Us'. Fay Weldon's 'anti-racist' recommendations are more than a little odd: apparently it is the *victims* of racism who must change, rather than their racist oppressors. It is really up to them, they should not make such targets of themselves. In Fay Weldon's book, 'monoculturalism' represents the *pragmatics* of the 'well-intentioned', while those who work within a *multicultural* paradigm remain 'paralysed' by *their* good intentions.

Fay Weldon's 'anti-racist' idiom differs symptomatically from ours in this book. Her good intentions, while doubtless good, are not ours. Take two paradigms, two sets of good intentions. Fay Weldon claims key concepts of the well-intentioned – justice, freedom, rights, equality – for a liberal-humanist paradigm which supposes *human* beings rather than *cultural* beings, human rights rather than cultural rights. This chapter, like others in the book, takes a different view. Identities, values and rights are at bottom *cultural* (material, disclosed, local), rather than *human* (abstract, mystified, deferred, universal). Thus, 'human' values are variously estimated, inter-culturally contested. What passes for 'human' is a matter of cultural hegemony, not 'nature'.

Liberal humanism thinks itself enlightened, free of myth and hearsay; it is too sure of itself to have truck with gods, prophets and canonical texts. But, as Fay Weldon suggests, liberal humanism is a 'religion' too:

> The God I recognise is the *ordinary human capacity* to feel joy and
> sorrow, hope and disappointment, in proper proportion; and with-

out let or hindrance: a sense of the transcendent . . .[20] (emphasis added).

The 'God' of liberal humanism is 'humanity', whose 'truths' the liberal humanist would have universally, or at least nationally, acknowledged. Liberal humanism is not without its prophets and canonical texts: certain authors are its prophets, the literature they write its canonical texts. In his recent book *Authors*, the zealous, revivalist hymn of a believer, Karl Miller notes 'our' assumptions about authors: 'We' think them '*humanly* and historically representative' (emphasis added), and there are some authors whom 'we' are disposed to worship.[21] For Karl Miller, some *chosen* authors – he does not say who does the choosing – are exceptional and strange: both anchored in culture, *and* able to soar free of its discursive localities. Like Mohammed and Jesus, *some* authors are prophets: they tell us human truths. The text of transcendental humanism is the literature that these authors write, and that their literary predecessors wrote. The literary canon is the humanist canon. We are advised to expose ourselves to it, revere it, learn timeless human truths from it. God is dead, so is Allah; long live the author.

Fay Weldon says the Qur'an is 'food for no-thought',[22] that all you can do with it is 'learn it by heart'.[23] Literature, on the other hand, Fay Weldon thinks, Salman Rushdie thinks, Karl Miller thinks, the Cox Committee thinks, the cultural engineers of 'Our' new nation think, is complex, ambiguous, subtle, manifoldly suggestive, good for you. But then Muslims always were suckers of nasty doctrine. They do not think, do they? Literature is for Christians and humanists, who do.

The views of those labelled – often from some considerable distance – 'multicultural' do not make the kind of common sense that is biting lately. Barely entertained in current hegemonic reckonings is a simple demand, simply expressed by a Muslim student I teach: 'We want the equal opportunities to be as we are'. The freedom, that is, of different cultural groups to maintain their identities, values and philosophies. The liberal humanist who threatens to curtail those freedoms, promising instead a greater, 'human' freedom, is culturally partisan rather than humanly representative. Liberal humanism is woolly sheep's clothing for very bourgeois wolves: it remains the ideological currency of Western, white, middle-class culture, or at least of powerful fractions of that class culture.

One such powerful fraction is the liberal intelligentsia, a formidable lobby with a loud, penetrating voice. The liberal intelligentsia networks into the quick of institutionalised power; it presses its point over dinner; it publishes and broadcasts its concerns: as Fay Weldon puts it, it holds its 'conversations' 'in public'.[24] The liberal intelligentsia is a useful friend, until it turns on you. Its members are generally good people, and they campaign, generally, on behalf of good causes. The right of Salman Rushdie to live an unthreatened, unmolested life *is* a right that needs to be campaigned for. How ironic, though, that in defending Salman Rushdie, a worthy thing to do, certain of Rushdie's colleagues have *indiscriminately* attacked Muslim culture in Britain. The defence of the human rights of one man has taken the form of threatening the cultural, *human* rights of thousands of his fellow citizens. This threat should not be underestimated, it is sustained by 'common sense': in Fay Weldon's *Sacred Cows*, in the Cox Report, in Government policy, and in other revisionist critiques of multiculturalism.

So what the good liberal giveth, they now wish to take away. But our multicultural society was not *given* in the first place – there was no first place – and is not available for snatching back in a moment of ideological doubt, or as a gesture of solidarity with a literary colleague. 'Multiculturalism' has become a favourite topic of liberal conversation, while the actualities and complexities of Britain's multicultural society go unmentioned. Britain's multicultural society is many different sets of local circumstances; it is *not* one 'thing' that can be said to have succeeded or failed.

'Multiculturalism' has been used constructively as a focus for those, particularly in education, working towards anti-racist practice. But it is a word easily manipulated – as it has been in *Sacred Cows* – to sound fragile, gormless, do-gooding and naïve, remote, as it often is in the discourse of liberal commentators, from the people and the circumstances that it allegedly denotes. In certain discursive usages, it sounds like a generic field of liberal endeavour, another modish 'ism' of social science. The instance of *Sacred Cows* shows that 'multiculturalism' is a term too easily ceded to, and claimed by, a liberal discourse, to become what Fay Weldon calls 'our conversations in public', conversations of which those labelled 'multicultural' are blank-faced referents, and *in* which they are *personae non gratae*. Somewhere beyond the approximation 'multiculturalism' are the lives that people lead, the beliefs that they hold, and the diverse politics of their manifold interactions. Such complex, heterogeneous circumstances have certainly *not* been permitted and arranged by 'the likes of myself': to suggest that they have writes out the self-determination of people who, though on the whole absent from centres of hegemonic power such as media institutions, are not mindlessly and uncritically plugged into 'our conversations in public'. The circumstances that are glossed by the term 'multiculturalism' have been evolved by those whose circumstances they are, not brought about by a pilot scheme of liberal thinkers who, a whiff of singed Literature in the air, declare multiculturalism *their* folly, a thing that *they* tried out, and that they atone for.

Multiculturalism as postmodernism

Certain radical-leftist fashionings of 'multiculturalism' have preferred metaphors that tell of surfaces and flatness: 'mosaic', 'patchwork', 'jigsaw'. Multiculturalism has always been in danger of neglecting the stories, genealogies, heirlooms and histories – the *depths* – of cultural groups, in favour of an optimistic pluralism: 'the quixotic notion that all positions in culture and politics are *now* open and equal'[25] (emphasis added). Multiculturalism tends to connote a gaze entranced by the aesthetics of cultural difference. And some critics of multiculturalism are right to deduce from the term a 'designer' politics: the narcissism of the politically 'right-on', fascinated by their own willingness to accept the maxim that 'anything goes'. Such tendencies have been challenged usefully by the practice and thinking of 'anti-racism',which has wanted to attend not merely to cultural difference for difference's sake, but to the politics that accrue at the thresholds of difference, to the cultural genealogies of different groups in Britain, to the depths beneath the surface.

If multiculturalism rests its case for a multicultural society on the maxim that difference is a good thing which ought to be celebrated, its language is easily turned inside out. If for some difference is good, simply that, then for others it is, just as simply, bad. Turning the jargon of multiculturalism inside out has been one of the strategies of the hegemonic project of cultural uniformity whose texts include Fay Weldon's *Sacred Cows*, and the Cox Report about which Professor Cox has spoken. It is to Professor Cox's lecture[26] that I would like to turn.

Professor Cox makes it clear that the underlying concern of the Cox Report, its 'unconscious' brief, is to address the issue of 'tension' in the national culture between 'unity' and 'diversity'. In this respect its calling is the same as Fay Weldon's. And Professor Cox did not let pass the opportunity to cite the Rushdie Affair as evidence of such 'tension'. Conceived, like *Sacred Cows*, as a 'healing' text, the Cox Report represents a principal contribution to the hegemonic 'conversation' about national identity. Yet it too denies its collusion with, and boasts its departure from, an undisclosed formulation of the 'dominant' or 'orthodox'. As Fay Weldon's publishers see fit to market their author's exhortations as 'dissidence', so Professor Cox has claimed for his Working Group's recommendations the epithet 'revolutionary'.[27]

By 'unity', Professor Cox means a 'common culture'; by 'diversity', the struggle of divergent cultural interests with not enough in common. Professor Cox feels that his committee's Report went some considerable way towards reconciling the two, to 'balancing' 'legitimate' arguments for national unity with those for a multicultural society, by making *one* culture available to everyone through access (he should have said *mandatory* access) to standard English and the canon (a protean one, he insisted) of English literature. All this to ensure that, culturally, people are not sufficiently different for their multicultural differences to become inflamed, for books to get burnt.

In his diagnosis of the condition of Britain, Professor Cox confuses two entirely separate paradigms, 'multiculturalism' and 'postmodernism', neither of which touches the 'grass roots' of Britain's multicultural society. He cites the divergences of Britain's multicultural society as the source of an 'identity crisis' that torments the nation, and the senses of 'self' of British nationals. Yet in order to prove that such a problem exists, Cox offers no specific instances of cultural malfunction (apart from an oblique reference to the Rushdie Affair) but instead draws selectively from paradigms of postmodernism for his list of symptoms. Exile; alienation; difference as 'spectacle'; the terrors of multiplicity; excessive pluralism; fragmentation; instability; displacement; historical amnesia; crises of subjectivity; cultural anarchy; and cultural relativism whose collective fault it is that people flock to the fundamentalisms of Islam and Christianity for consolation and certainty. Professor Cox's list includes all of those. He appropriates the themes of various postmodernisms and ascribes them wholesale to multiculturalism as proof that the latter has gone wrong, and that something needs to be done. He seizes cultural symptoms –

'schizophrenia', fragmentation – wrought, according to certain postmodernisms though Cox doesn't acknowledge this, by capitalist production,[28] and blames multiculturalism for them. Cox's alarm only works in a false paradigm – multiculturalism-cum-postmodernism – in which he conceives the politics of multiculturalism as the poetics of postmodernism. He is a very long way from Britain's 'polyglot, miscegenated and international *realities*'.[29]

The correspondence between a multicultural society and postmodernism is, at a push, allegorical, no more than that. But by deducing a 'multicultural problematic' from the discursive shards of a range of theories that have gone under the generic heading 'postmodernism', Professor Cox finds a way of justifying the Cox Report's campaign of cultural reformation as therapy for cultural 'ills'. The nation is sick because 'We' lack 'totality' in our lives. The Cox Report seeks to foster what 'We' so badly 'need': unity; coherence; continuity; connection; security; relationship; roots; tradition; heritage.

It suits the advocate of a common culture to dwell on the multicultural surface without looking beneath it for the different histories and heritages of people in Britain. A common cultural future, the optimism of the National Curriculum suggests, can be legislated for; but many pasts have already happened, and those that trouble the nation's hegemonic sense of itself are best forgotten. The new English wants *all* school students to 'recall' *one* 'national' past. 'Pastoral continuity', healer of multicultural ills, hegemonic attempt to call all of us to national heel, is to be fostered by exposing everyone to the canon of English literature and insisting that *it* is our heritage. Children, Professor Cox maintains, do need continuity.[30]

Quite so. Don't we all? But the ethnocentric programme of the 'new', 'revolutionary' English affords rather more continuity for some than others. For some students, the 'When in Rome' principle is to govern their alloted experience of school: there, they are to be interpellated by a curriculum that displaces the different senses of 'self' that have developed in the home and elsewhere, those 'extra-curricular' spaces that the Cox Report is not concerned with. There is precious little 'continuity' for them. Quite the opposite. Some students are required to lead a 'schizophrenic', a 'postmodern', cultural life. At school they must 'be' one thing: home is where the 'Other' is.

Multiculturalism as range

What are the literary texts of the new English that the nation's young have been granted mandatory access to? Few are cited in the Report. Cox's canon is a coy canon, but no less a canon for that. The fact that Shakespeare gets a paragraph of adulation all to himself in the section on literature[31] speaks the rest of the traditional canon's volumes. Where Shakespeare goes, the rest follow. The National Curriculum provides examples of the rest:

> Pupils should be introduced to . . . some of the works which have been most influential in shaping and refining the English language and its literature, eg. the Authorised Version of the Bible, Wordsworth's poems, or the novels of Austen, the Brontes or Dickens.[32]

Complete the list, and there's the traditional canon. 'Works which have been most influential in shaping and refining the English language and its literature' is a new-English euphemism for the 'Great Tradition', whose 'first flowers' remain masonically recommended as 'good literature': as instances of 'memorable language and interesting content . . . the distinguishing features of good quality texts'.[33] The 'best that has been thought and said', no doubt. But 'best' for whom?

The canon according to Cox is open and protean. It has its core, but is amenable to social and cultural diversity',[34] and it anticipates the charge of ethnocentrism by declaring a commitment to the concept of 'range'. It is prepared to treat cultural difference *in its terms*. The new English prides itself on its 'open access'. It is all things to all men, women, and other groups: everyone can find something of themselves and their interests there, and should succumb to its terms in order that they might 'understand more of themselves'.[35] Literature is universal and anticipates the cultural condition of us all.

If the Cox Report is reticent, as MacCabe complains, about naming authors, it is more forthcoming about how the 'range' ought to be read. Coxian literature is there to help. It focuses the interests of different groups; moreover, 'critical thinking about existing stereotypes and values can be stimulated by studying *literature which expresses alternative points of view*'[36] (emphasis added). So much suggests the *peaceable correspondence* of some groups to some texts – tidy interpellations of those groups by those texts – and neglects the question of, say, black students studying

Conrad within the paradigm of English that is advocated. Literature according to this model is the *means*, not the *object*, of cultural critique. That's what Leavis said Literature was. And Cox's Literature, like Leavis', offers us 'alternative' views of 'the family, nature and industrialisation'.[37] The list is more than a little dated, the 'radicalism' of Leavis rather tame in Cox.

For a text whose mission is to address Britain's multicultural 'problematic', the Cox Report's discussion of literature does not get far. Incumbent multiculturalism is provided for by 'range'. The multicultural 'beast' is pacified, patronised, patted on its various heads. There is no sense of a dominant culture with which 'different' groups interact dialectically, no sense of the unequal power relations of difference. Along with men, women, and adolescents, bound by their apparently commensurate 'differences', 'minorities of different kinds' must scan the canon's range for 'other' texts sympathetic to them so that *they too* can become programmed by the 'moral technology' that is literature.[38] Then everyone will be able to ' "grow" through literature – both emotionally and aesthetically, both morally and socially'.[39] But not politically. The new English, like the old English, holds the politics of culture in abeyance. Its paradigm is a *human, universal* one, not a *cultural* one. For Cox, cultural difference is a local detail of our binding humanity.

The canon's assimilation of 'other' texts is similar to the hegemonic desire to make people of 'other' cultural denominations fully-fledged members of the new national 'We', to extend to them the national-cultural franchise. If 'literary' is a way of 'placing' texts, 'national' is a way of 'placing' people. The 'literary' and the 'national' assimilate texts and cultures only to disavow the cultural, political 'memory' of each. It is the hegemonic project of the new nation and the new literature to embrace rather than exclude: to rope the 'Other' in. But only so that the voice of the 'Other' – text and culture – is reduced to a whisper. English, its dominant tradition alive in the Coxian paradigm, makes space for 'other' voices and 'other' texts only to patronise their ethnicity. A classic instance of this is the canon's ambivalent embrace of what it has called 'magic realism', appropriated as a bit of the 'Other' to titillate the dull canon and extend its tenure. It is that kind of annexation that 'range' provides for. Cox's canon is multicultural in these terms:

English teachers should seek opportunities to exploit the

multicultural aspects of literature. Novels from India or Caribbean
poetry might be used for study of differing cultural perspectives, for
example. Not only should this lead to a broader awareness of a
greater range of human 'thought and feeling', but – through looking
at literature from different parts of the world and written from
different points of view – pupils should also be in a position to gain a
better understanding of the cultural heritage of English literature
itself.[40]

Note the lack of curiosity about the conditions under which the
multicultural writing up for grabs was produced. That is what
comes of rendering something *literary* and part of a *human* scheme.
Yet a good deal of Commonwealth writing, much of it favoured by
the canon – was not written *as* English literature but rather *in
opposition to* the cultural hegemony that English literature has
always represented. It is at the very least audacious for the canon,
hegemonic apparatus of a white, colonising class fraction, to help
itself to writing that was often produced in conscientious opposition to that class fraction, only to deny the political and cultural
conditions of its origins by universalising it as text of the 'human'
condition.

English: the wrong subject
English, as hegemonic design has traditionally disposed it, is where
the white middle-class auditions members of other cultural groups
for parts in *its* cultural scene. Graduation into that scene guarantees
'social betterment', makes you better.[41] To 'succeed', to get the part,
you must become an actor, a masquerader, a parvenu, an *arriviste*.
It seems to me this describes the trajectories of a good many English
teachers, the cultural dialectics of whose biographies might well
inhibit their willingness to come quietly and carry out the 'greatest
joys' of their job as Cox expects them to.

In the main, Cox is pleased with the way English teachers are
rising to the challenge of the New English,[42] but he has doubts
about some of them. A cause of concern are those who, as
undergraduates, attended *ideologically* rather than discerningly
towords. The 'New Theory' – structuralism, feminism, psychoanalysis, poststructuralism, Marxism – has produced an English-
teaching fraction, or faction, of sceptics and non-believers who are
themselves symptoms of the 'cultural uncertainty' Cox says plagues
the nation. Can *those* English teachers be trusted to promote

Coxian 'common culture', carry out the 'positive task', and evangelise the goodness of the literary text?

No they can't. And for various good reasons (I cite my own). I am one of the 'young teachers' Cox worries about, who, as undergraduates, were as interested in what he calls the 'poststructuralist canon' as the literary one. And yes, I *was* more interested in those approaches that sought to call literature to cultural account, address its cultural politics, than in those that advocated '*belles-lettristic* preciosity' and 'gush about sunsets'.[43]

English literature, its fundamentalists claim, represents a 'greater' democracy, an escape from culture. The Oxbridge don Marilyn Butler, active in a campaign to restore literature to its 'rightful eminence' in schools, puts it like this:

> Some schools think literature is a subject that posh kids do. We are trying to persuade them it is a democratic subject which lets people escape from narrow circumstances.[44]

If you are not a member of the class fraction that corresponds aboriginally to literary culture, you're in chains: incapable of thinking, reasoning and behaving freely. 'Freedom' is to be found in the universal, human wisdoms of literary culture. To be 'truly' free, 'aculturally' free, you must graduate into that culture, and discard your own 'narrow circumstances'. Literature refuses to leave you where you were. Converts must be upwardly mobile. It makes of those from 'narrow circumstances' displaced persons.

Before I reached university my 'relationship' with literature was a source of cultural discomfort. Coming from 'narrow circumstances' (though their horizons seemed, still seem, magnificently broad to me) I was obliged to feign a liberal-humanist sensibility in order to gain 'access' to it. To pass the A level, I learned the codes of literary 'feeling'. I wrote poignantly enough about Tess pulling swedes until her fingers bled, and went without knowing about rural economy in nineteenth-century England – its wandering 'proletariat', the insecurity of employment, the legacies of enclosure, the status of working women – and its (mis)representations in discourses of rusticity.

The early 1980s saw the New Theory settle itself factionally in English departments where it put the wind up the liberal-humanist establishment, for whose ideologues Derrida was the devil, come to deride. The New Theory meant you did not have to *care* about 'art' and *feel* for 'literature', it meant you could stop pretending. Instead, you were invited to go to work on texts with methodologies that challenged the very status and hegemony of 'literature', and made space for the political articulation of your own cultural interests. For the non-middle-class malcontent, forced to pay false homage to Leavisism and liberal humanism, such methodologies provided a 'pragmatics' for scepticism that had seemed to smack of class jealousy, humanistic inadequacy, academic weakness, looney-leftness, or chips on shoulders. For many whose passage to English required, as mine did, 'escaping' from 'narrow circumstances', the struggle between 'Literature' and Theory was a class struggle.

There is a 'We' that I have kept in quotation marks in this chapter: the 'We' of consensus, that of Coxian common culture. The real *we* live (not live*s*) in a society that exploits and discriminates against people because of their race, their class, their religion, their sexuality and their gender. We cannot and should not be culturally homogenous: 'A divided society should have a divided culture: an (apparently) unified culture can only reinforce power relations'.[45] The second part of that sentence describes the hegemonic programme that the Cox Report has contributed to.

It is not the cultures of oppressed groups that should change, but rather the perception that 'difference' carries deficit and threat. 'Equal opportunities' is a term that has been hijacked by the Right to denote 'access' to the dominant culture, 'enfranchisement' in its terms, rather than the freedom to be different. 'Difference' is not the same as 'division'. A multicultural society is not necessarily a divided one. Difference from each other is what we have in common. Upholding the maxim that 'the British way of life consists of a variety of ways of life', the Commission for Racial Equality has expressed its commitment to 'an ideal of a pluralist society in which *cultural diversity is seen as a source of unity* not as a "problem"'[46] (emphasis added).

Genuinely common to us all is a curriculum that allows students, in their investigations of texts, to discover something of the *many* heritages and identities of Britain, not just the parochial, white, bourgeois *one*. The production of knowledge is an acutely political business, as the hidden agenda of the National Curriculum illustrates. The National Curriculum seeks to fortify the dominant culture by assimilating other cultures, the 'Other', in order to make its *own* culture impregnably common, that of the new One Nation, of *one* this, *one* that. It is in the common interests of most of us, the

'Others', to work towards the transformation of an existing order that allows dominant groups to play nasty and nice at hegemonic whim: to kick us around one minute, and rope us in the next.

'Make of me a man who questions' ,[47] wrote Frantz Fanon, in whose political interests it most certainly was to question. In its commitment to stability and continuity – that is, the maintenance of existing power relations – the National Curriculum in English proscribes questions of the kind Fanon has in mind. It allows precious little flexibility for teachers, and hardly any opportunity for 'new knowledges', *different* stories, to be produced. It prefers the same old stories. Better than what went before? Yes, if you want a 'set of rigid rules for living, perceiving and thinking'.[48]

But in its eagerness to provide one, official knowledge, the new English deprives its subject-students of 'skills' whose development it is the duty of the teacher to foster. The new English does not theorise the cognitive value of its provision. Politically disturbing an investigative, questioning approach to language and literature might be for some, but at least such an approach promises the production of a range of knowledges, and the formation of conceptual structures missing in the Coxian model. *Literary* studies of *Jane Eyre* have no trouble reading a mad woman in the attic, a Gothic 'extra'. But, in another curricular scene, Bertha Mason's 'mirthless laughter' begs questions about the 'confinement' of middle-class Victorian women, about the cultural dialectics of colonised Jamaica, about the colonial unconscious – or conscience – of conspicuous wealth in nineteenth-century England. Those are *useful* knowledges. As well as entertaining a feminist account of history, and entertaining black heritages along with white ones, the second scene fosters a learning experience of far superior quality to the first.

Arguing against the scene of Coxian English, I am advocating not that its texts be scrapped, but that they be redeployed, along with other cultural artefacts, in a different scene, where they might yield different, various stories, knowledges, theories, histories and values. A scene, that is, in which investigations of texts, and of the cultural dialectics necessarily available in them, involve realisations, rather than disavowals, of *different* cultural perspectives, *those of the different investigators.*

There is not space here to detail the curricular largesse required for a pedagogic scene of genuine multicultural integrity. In brief, my position is that, in schools, cultural studies ought to supercede

English. Certain progressive departments in higher education have
taken the lead. Opposed to the kind of 'idealism' that vitiates the
Cox Report, Jonathan Dollimore and Alan Sinfield, extending the
legacy of Raymond Williams, argue for the practice of 'cultural
materialism': 'a combination of historical and cultural context,
theoretical method, political commitment and textual analysis'.[49]
Without those curricular permissions, stranded in the literary
paradigm, instilling still, dead knowledge, old, old stories, year in
year out, the teaching of texts like Conrad's *Heart of Darkness*, as I
illustrate below, represents a preposterous task. [50]

Teaching *Heart of Darkness*: the white man's burden
'They *must* be represented'.[51] And they have been. Women by men;
blacks by whites; East by West; the unliterary by the literary; the
tongue-tied by quick, forked tongues that always have their say,
their conversations in public.

In *Heart of Darkness*, black Africans are represented by and for
white Europe. That is the colonial way. Whites do the representing;
it is for non-whites to be represented – they *must* be represented.

I, a white teacher of 'A' level English literature, taught *Heart of
Darkness* recently in a white institution – a college of further
education in Tottenham, north London, to a group of 22 students
of whom some 18 were non-white, and of those most were Afro-
Caribbean. According to Cox, they *must* be taught.

The pedagogic scene I found myself acting in reproduces the
colonial relationship, of which *Heart of Darkness* is a notorious
document. The verb has changed – then, to represent now, to teach
about those representations – but still the active subject of the verb
is white, the passive object black. The occasion – *Literature* – on
which white subject and black object encounter each other at the
verb also remains the same. Conrad's book is a pristine example of
colonial literature. These days it is the canon's darling. These days,
the 'positive task' of English teaching represents a neo-colonial
task, that of forcing 'them' to commune with 'our' culture, by
playing parts in the finely-scripted scene of English, so that they'll
forget themselves and become more like us. 'We' forced our
language and literature on 'them' when we were over there; now
that they are over here – because we were over there – the same
thing is happening, albeit somewhat less brutally. The colonial
relation remains in place. To enfold people in the cultural superiority of English remains the white man's burden.

To reproduce colonial relations in the teaching of a colonial text whitewashes two active, historically distinct, but genealogically and politically related, cultures – that of the represented, and that of the taught – leaving them untold, disavowed, estranged. To foster an encounter between represented and taught is to entertain the (multi)cultural politics of reading, an entitlement of students, anathema to Cox. To keep them estranged, as English must, perpetuates a great white lie.

Kehinde, a black student whom Suzanne Scafe engaged in conversation, recognises the neo-colonial tendencies of English, and realises that liberating herself from 'object' of the colonial verb, accentuating learning rather than teaching, activating her own history, calls for a different curricular scene. In response to Suzanne Scafe's question 'What made you decide to study English?' Kehinde has this to say:

> English literature? I dunno. I dunno why I'm doing it. I wanted to do Black history really. I want to know more Black history but it wouldn't be recognised in the exam. . . . I don't want white teachers teaching me about Black people anyway. You should go about learning your own way. You should learn yourselves by teaching yourselves. They go to the West Indies and Africa, teaching us about ourselves, but they'd teach us in a way that would control us.[52]

Anti-racist though we might consider our practice as English teachers, Kehinde puts me, a white English teacher of *Heart of Darkness*, full of good, anti-racist intentions, firmly in my place: that of a white missionary, a neo-colonial agent. Given script, scene and actors as I have detailed them, for A-level English it is apparently the white man's current burden to teach black students about the white man's former burden. Not much promise of anti-racist, or even non-racist, practice there.

Within the paradigm of English literature, white teacher typically at the controls, 'anti-racist' readings of *Heart of Darkness* are indebted, rather like Fay Weldon's 'multicultural' society, to liberal, white permission. Such readings too easily become sentimental ponderings, abstract estimations of human rights, grist to the mill of Coxian humanism, rather than critical investigations of the *politics of representation* in colonial discourse.

As Kehinde makes clear, it is not for white teachers to 'un-pack' the tropes of colonial discourse before a black audience. It is not for me to act out my self-righteous fantasies of anti-racism in a

classroom full of black 'extras', as if auditioning for a part in one of
Richard Attenborough's 'anti-racist' epics.

Frantz Fanon wrote: 'There is a fact: white men consider
themselves superior to black men'.[53] Declaring myself an exception
does not mean there is 'no problem here'. English teachers are
bound, in spite of themselves, to collude with institutional racism,
embedded in Cox's English, and in institutions of education, whose
agents they *must* be.[54]

If genuinely anti-racist exegeses of texts such as *Heart of
Darkness* are to be performed in schools and colleges, white
teachers need to decentre and efface themselves, instead of trying to
'black up'. The prominence of their sympathy, liberal permissions
and efforts at empathy is unwelcome. They must be extras, they
must not take leading roles.

Heart of Darkness racist? In my view, undoubtedly. Should it be
withdrawn from syllabuses? The banal position of too many
fundamentalists of English literature is that *Heart of Darkness*
must be read (that imperative, again) precisely because it is a jewel
in the canon's rusting crown. It is 'good' literature, the literary
heritage, they lie, of all.

Of course, not reading *Heart of Darkness* (for many, a boring,
turgid book) is hardly likely to stunt the cognitive, intellectual and
cultural development of any student if he or she is reading
something else in its place. Reading this text always entails the lost
opportunity of reading that one. We might wonder at the *excessive*
presence of *Heart of Darkness* on English literature syllabuses; we
might consider, with due scepticism, the disproportionate efforts of
so many liberal-left academics to maintain that presence.

But while *what* is read is important, *how* texts are read is more so.
Bickering about the inventory of the canon, a misguided pastime of
too many on the left, actually works *for* the canon, preserving the
myth of inherent quality which can be recognised by those with taste.
Canonising other, 'new' texts is hardly progressive: if the canon shifts
its ground a bit, it is only in order to make itself more settled.
Bickering about what the canon should include, and exclude, leaves
unposed far more urgent questions: those of the pedagogic scenes in
which texts are 'read'; those of the kinds and range of knowledge,
conceptual thinking and roles for students that are rendered
potential by teaching a text in this scene rather than that one.

My own view is that *Heart of Darkness* can be useful, not as
Literature, but in the pursuit of colonial discourse.

Heart of Darkness is a fraught, white fantasy. Its metaphors are far more telling and enduring than any 'thesis' that might be attributed to it. 'Darkness' in the book figures as a key modernist anxiety: nothing within, the metaphysic of human interiority (which Cox wants to cultivate in students of English) apocalyptically discredited. 'Darkness' is also, rather more palpably, the black African: his skin, his sin, his deeds. The two themes – modernist crisis, and the African – are smudged together in the dark: each mystifies and confirms the other in a spiral of colonial panic. European bourgeois angst – moral, sexual, epistemological – is figured as, confessed as, and played out upon, the naked black body of the African. In that transference is to be found the ignition of colonial fantasy.

Heart of Darkness racist? If the book is the sum of its parts – and the cumulative 'deposits' of a text easily signify out of the control of, and often in opposition to, any deduced 'thesis' – readers encounter page upon page of 'nigger' this, 'savage' that, and 'brute' the other, without a single black point-of-view or other-than-bodily black presence. Black is white's pre-cultural, chaotic other. It is excessive, threatening, somatic, riskily sexual. It is desired and feared; shape and shadow; dangerous to know. And it might engulf or even eat you, a familiar colonial fantasy, as Frantz Fanon acknowledged: 'Mama,' cries a little white boy, 'the nigger's going to eat me up'.[55] Or beat me up, or mug me, or rape me, or rip me off, in current, neo-colonial fantasies.

Heart of Darkness transcribes the colonial structure whose reproduction I risked when I taught the book. Black is the scene of – it serves as the *mise-en-scène* for – Conrad's thoroughly white story. Imagine it as a film. There is a genre of film adaptations of those novels of Agatha Christie's set in colonial situations, typically Palestine earlier this century. Palestinians are cast as Enigma. Exotic, inscrutable, half-lit, unwholesome, they serve as 'extras' to thrill a white, parochial whodunnit. The whodunnit gets its generic 'atmosphere' of mystery and risk from the Orientalised face of the Arab. (The colonial gaze is *variously* fascinated: it makes its fantastic capital out of the *face* of the Arab, but out of the body of the African.) As in *Heart of Darkness* the 'evil' is exclusively European while Africans are there to provide an ominous *mise-en-scène* for its exposure; in the Agatha Christie films it is always a European who 'dunnit'. The point, though, is this: while all the white characters, save the guilty one, are vindicated, the Arab remains suspect, as the African must in *Heart of Darkness*. Colonial discourse will have Arab and African no other way.

True, the 'sickness' of the European ivory-grabbers and the hypocrisy of their missionary posturing are there in *Heart of Darkness*. But, ultimately, the 'savagery' lured from the depths of the European bourgeois psyche 'is' the black 'savage' of Africa. Such fantastical 'reproductions' of colonial subject-peoples are both theme and embarrassment of colonial discourse, as becomes clear if you consider colonial texts historically and comparatively. *Heart of Darkness* is not peculiar; it is typical. *Literary* criticism, meanwhile, gazes at it, usually with approbation, and comes up with what it pleases: there is an equal opportunities policy embedded in *Mein Kampf* if you stare at its tropes in a literary vacuum for long enough. Treating *Heart of Darkness* as a *literary* text stuns it, tames it, avoids it, loses it. 'Literature' likes to keep the peace, and usually succeeds in doing so.

To claim *Heart of Darkness* is not racist is like saying *The Satanic Verses* is really inoffensive to Muslims. If you take offence, you are irrational and impulsive (or stupid) when you ought to be getting to grips sensibly with the text, which, its apologists suspect, you have not read, or at least not 'properly'. Of course, in order to find your way to the 'benign' authorial view, you need *literary* skills, and faith in the availability in texts of authorial intention as 'meaning'. But that is another bitter debate. The points here are these. Literary texts, as the case of *The Satanic Verses* has shown, transmit very *unliterary* signals when freed from the jealous clutches of those guardians of literature who would restrain those signals. Furthermore, it is a bit rich to expect, as Cox does, those groups whose cultures, religions and histories have been plundered by producers and reproducers of literature to have a vested interest in preserving the sanctity of literature. Literature has rarely done *them* justice. It is in the interests of 'referred-to' groups, descendents of the silent represented, those who would now be taught, to make the cultural stuff of literature their business *outside* the literary paradigm, that is, to claim an 'independent critical acquaintance' with literature. It should not be forgotten that, recently, literature's referred-to 'Other' did just that, springing, as it were, from the literary text to torch it. Those with Coxian tendencies should consider themselves warned.

Meanwhile, there are students whose potential anger is blocked by anxiety to pass A-level English. The students I taught had not read the 93 Penguin pages of *Heart of Darkness* before we came to tackle it together in class. They said it was too difficult and too boring.

The beginning is not a good place to begin. The first few pages give a gloomy, half-lit scene where 'We' are introduced to several characters who are soon discarded – all but one, that is, who embarks on a story that removes 'Us' to another narrative dimension. It is confusing. Allow your eye to miss a few words and you have missed the switch, and, before you know it, the *Nellie*, a 'cruising yawl', is cruising down the Congo.

The English teacher's job is to 'sensitise' students to the language of the book – the AEB 652 syllabus calls for their 'response' to it. The language of *Heart of Darkness* is densely metaphorical and as, after all, the metaphor is the message, I felt the least I could do was work towards some kind of discussion about how the structures of racism that colonial discourse manufactures as 'knowledge' embed themselves in symptomatic metaphors. The imaginary can't work without metaphor. It is through the 'logic' of metaphor that 'irrational' links and 'undue' associations are forged and, as particular metaphors become archetypes of discourse, naturalised.

I typed out an appropriate section from the book. There is something happily unliterary about a single sheet of home-type with mistakes. Students were easily able to circle references to 'black' and 'darkness', and box anything to do with 'light' and 'white'. They did this in pairs. Inking their own grid of critical authority onto the text at the outset seemed to defuse the mistrustful air in the room: mistrustful of the book and me.

I listed each pair's findings on the board, and asked what the relationship was between squares and circles. 'Different', 'enemies', 'opposites', came the responses. Next, as a whole class, people shouting out, we noted other expressions or words that have white/light or black/dark as their base. Examples I recorded are 'enlighten', 'to shed light on something', 'white lie', 'black look', 'black comedy', 'dark deeds', 'black as night'. No connection was made with 'race' at this stage. Back in pairs, students came up with scenarios or slices of narrative that made 'sense' of those expressions. We ended up with a list of connotations for each of the binary partners 'white' and 'black'. In the light/white column were 'knowable', 'safe', 'clean', 'warm','visible', 'torch', 'illuminate'; while the dark/black column had 'night', 'fear', 'blind','danger', 'horror film', 'confused', 'thriller'.

I explained to the class that we had identified chains of associations whose items trigger one another off in people's imaginations. When one word or expression from the column is used, the rest of the column is, in spite of the user, potentially suggested. Similarly, the items of each column trigger their opposites from the other. What we say exceeds what we mean to say. Metaphor holds together chains of associations. Get to know the kinds of associations that it naturalises, and you have gained an insight into the ideological metabolisms of a discourse.

This preparatory work done, it proved easier to realise the effects (discursive, not literary) of metaphor in the book as a whole. Students became adept at discussing ways in which links between 'black' and 'darkness' metaphorically collapse together the African non-characters and the African landscape. One student suggested that Conrad *hides* Africa in swathes of metaphor, that he had a 'problem' with Africa, it vexed him, and that the book is 'difficult' and 'boring' for that reason – the author's fault, not the student's, that it should appear so.

The metaphor work was successful up to a point. And that point lies on the boundary of what conventionally goes as school English. If you try to take the work further, you have a boundary dispute on your hands: you are over the border into history, geography, philosophy, politics. It is not enough simply to provide a space for black students, any students, to trace chains of associations, the 'bottom line' of racist discourse, at the fundamental level of language. If you do this, and nothing more, you leave the impression that language was always racist, and always will be. It will not do merely to expose the rules and codes of racist language forms without investigating *why* they are as they are. If you shirk, or are prevented from attempting, this, you leave in place a tautology – it is, because it is – and thus you leave the 'lesson' unfinished. You leave a sense of powerlessness before the 'inevitabilities' of language.

One way of taking the work further is to situate the metaphors in history, to return to colonial discourse the agency, materiality and genealogy it pretends it does not have. The provenance of colonial discourse is distributed over many forms, many disciplines: paintings, parliamentary speeches, children's literature, history text books, 'boy's own' literature. All available, and easily imported into classrooms. As an isolated text, *Heart of Darkness* is useless. Useful knowledge is available at its edges, and at the edges of the English paradigm – or, rather, just over them, in the interstices, where English and other subject paradigms are so coy about the possibility of touching one another that they do not touch. Subject disciplines are notoriously territorial, and it is in the perceived interests of many subject 'experts' to keep it that way.

Colonial discourse of the *Heart of Darkness* brand and racist idiom in Britain today are genealogically related and structurally similar. To engineer a useful encounter between text and students, that is, between represented and taught, an investigation of colonial discourse needs, at the same time and within a whole methodology, to intervene in *current* discourses of racism, whose 'texts', often, are students' testimonies of their own first-hand experiences. A good starting point for this dual investigation is *representation.*

Heart of Darkness, whose metaphoricity is above all excessive and 'illogical', provides a seminal instance of colonial-racialist stereotyping in accordance with Homi Bhabha's observation that the stereotype must always be 'in excess of what can be empirically proved or logically construed'. The easy dismissal of *Heart of Darkness* as 'racist', and the withdrawal of it from syllabuses, while motivated by anti-racism, is not necessarily a shrewd move. Bhabha warns against knee-jerk, spot-the-stereotype approaches to the study of texts:

> My reading of colonial discourse suggests that the point of interven-tion should shift from the *identification* of images as either positive or negative, to an understanding of the *process of subjectification* made possible (and plausible) through stereotypical discourse.[56]

Bhabha cites the film *A Touch of Evil*, to demonstrate his point. Image-analysis has been prolific in its investigations of stereotypical discourse, both in film studies and its schismatic off-shoot Media Studies. In Media Studies, GCSE and 'A' level, 'decoding' ster-eotypes through semiotic analysis of media images is regarded as the ABC of the subject. Colonial discourse is words *and* pictures: its coherence is realised across the two. It is regrettable that, mostly in schools and colleges, words and pictures belong to different paradigms and usually different subjects.

'A whirl of black limbs', 'a black and incomprehensible frenzy', 'black shadows', 'loitering presences'. Representations, all, of black people, lifted from *Heart of Darkness*. If I said I had lifted the last two from tabloid treatments of the Brixton Riots 10 years ago, I

would scarcely be disbelieved. The colonial 'process of subjectification' has proved enduring. There is no shortage of paranoid tabloid
representations – words and pictures anchoring each other to seal
the 'process of subjectification' – of black people in contemporary
Britain. These representations are direct descendents of those
deposited in the pages of *Heart of Darkness*. The colonial stereotype is deployed against 'Them' now they are over here. There is a
veritable genre in which black men are represented as night-
prowlers in the urban 'jungle': potential muggers, sexually threatening (and fascinating, of course); mad, black, and dangerous to
know.

Teaching *Heart of Darkness*, I could not fail to notice that
students who did Media Studies were far more able to challenge
textual representations of black people than those who did not.
Encouraged to demonstrate their Media Studies skills, these
students seemed more *comfortable* investigating the text: Media
Studies is more 'user-friendly' than literature; its texts are usually
students' own; its research is usually in *their* cultural interests.

Practical criticism and literary criticism collude with the literary
bureaucracies of the literary text. *Semiotic* analyses of 'word
images' acknowledge literary 'signifiers', but, more importantly, are
able to estimate the cultural generation of typical language forms.
Semiotic analysis makes some attempt, at least, to separate cultural
wood from literary trees. Students equipped with the skills Media
Studies normally fosters were ready to think semiotically (con-
notatively) past the literary codes and bureaucracies of *Heart of
Darkness*.

Pictures were missing from our study. Their inclusion would
have enhanced and vindicated students' semiotic skills. A consideration of words and pictures together suggests that what is being
investigated is neither 'literature' nor 'media', but *discourse*, which
is to be found in correspondences across and among texts, not as an
'essence' of them.

Most A-level English literature syllabuses that include *Heart of
Darkness*, certainly the AEB 652 syllabus, insist that students gaze
lengthily, preferably with approbation,at that literary text. The
'unliterary' approach recommended by Jonathan Dollimore and
Alan Sinfield (above) invites the student's gaze to wander to the
edges of the text, and beyond, in pursuit of colonial discourse.
Reading *Heart of Darkness* in relation to other colonial representations of its time, and in relation to examples of 'neo-colonial'

racialist discourse, goes some way towards addressing Kehinde's grievances. Students are granted the curricular space to bring to an academic context their *personal* experiences and knowledge of the racialist 'process of subjectification', and to consider its antecedents.

There is no space for the *personal* in English, only the 'personal', that dainty, white, middle-class persona that isolates itself from the social and from the political. To enlist the genuinely personal participation of students in investigations of texts devolves the production of *political* meaning, a necessary effect of encounters between students and texts, from teachers onto students. Teaching *Heart of Darkness* thus, the white man is relieved of his burden.

Notes

1. Professor Cox made this point in one of a series of lectures , 'Politics anda National Curriculum in English', University College London, 20 February 1991.
2. Fay Weldon, *Sacred Cows*, 1989, p. 31.
3. John Casey, 'One Nation: The Politics of Race', *Salisbury Review*, no. 1 (1982).
4. The term is Jacques Derrida's.
5. *The European* (12 February 1991)
6. Ibid.
7. *The Observer* 23 September 1990.
8. *The Sport* (22 January 1991)
9. *Sunday Express* 2 July 1989.
10. Fay Weldon, *Sacred Cows*, 1989, publishers' blurb on back cover.
11. Ibid., p. 20.
12. Ibid., p. 33.
13. Ibid., p. 31.
14. Ibid., p. 29.
15. Ibid., p. 33.
16. Ibid., p. 32.
17. Ibid., p. 32.
18. Ibid., p. 34.
19. Ibid., p. 38.
20. Ibid., p. 11.
21. Karl Miller, *Authors*, 1989, p. 163.
22. Fay Weldon, *Sacred Cows*, 1989, p. 6.
23. Ibid., p. 33.
24. Ibid., p. 13.
25. Hal Foster (ed.) *Postmodern Culture*, 1983, p. xi.
26. University College London, 20 February 1991.
27. *Critical Quarterly*, 32, 4, Winter 1990, p. 2.

28. See Frederic Jameson's essay 'Post Modernism or the Cultural Logic of Late Capitalism', *New Left Review*, 146, July/August 1984.

29. The phrase is from a *Critical Quarterly* publicity leaflet. *Critical Quarterly*, of which Professor Cox is a general editor, has declared its commitment to analysing those very realities.

30. For a more detailed response to Professor Cox's lecture, see Anne Turvey's chapter in this book.

31. 'English for Ages 5 to 16' ('Cox') 1989, para. 7. 16.

32. NC programmes of study for reading; key stages 3 and 4; 15.

33. English non-statutory guidance: 1.3.

34. Cox, 7.4.

35. Ibid., 7.3.

36. Ibid., 7.4.

37. Ibid., 7.4.

38. The term is Terry Eagleton's, in Suzanne Scafe, *Teaching Black Literature*, 1989, p. 77.

39. Cox, 7.3.

40. Cox 7.5.

41. Clara Connolly has written: 'There's an old and tenacious tradition in England which has it that education is central to the process of social betterment, and that English is itself the key discipline in this. It is also a profoundly ideological tradition which must be rejected', *English Teaching and Class*, Kean (ed.) ILEA, 1989.

42. He said as much in his lecture at University College London, 20 February 1991.

43. Terry Eagleton, *Literary Theory*, 1983.

44. *The Independent on Sunday*, 10 February 1991.

45. Alan Sinfield, *Literature, Culture and Politics in Postwar Britain*, 1989, p. 300.

46. *Swann: A Response from the Commission for Racial Equality*, 1985, p. 1.

47. Frantz Fanon, *Black Skin, White Masks*, 1986, p. 12.

48. The words are Fay Weldon's, her assessment of the Qur'an, *Sacred Cows*, 1989, p. 5.

49. In John Barrell, *Poetry, Language and Politics*, 1988, p. vii.

50. What I go on to describe is A-level teaching. Although the National Curriculum does not, at least at the time of writing, concern post-16 education, A level is the area of English teaching that has benefited least from the radical-progressivism (the 'egalitarianism') of some school English over the last 20 years. The paradigm of most A-level syllabuses is close to that of Cox.

51. Karl Marx's words; Edward Said uses them to introduce his book *Orientalism*, 1978.

52. Suzanne Scafe, *Teaching Black Literature*, 1989, p. 11.

53. Franntz Fanon, *Black Skin, White Masks*, 1986, p. 12.
54. The Commission for Racial Equality endorsed the distinction in the Swann Report between individual prejudice and institutional racism: 'Institutional racism operates through the normal workings of the system rather than the conscious intent of the prejudiced individual' *Swann: A Response . . .*, 1985, p. 1.
55. Frantz Fanon, *Black Skin, White Masks*, 1986, p. 114.
56. Homi Bhabha in *Literature, Politics and Theory*, Francis Barker *et al.* (eds), 1986, p. 149.

Afterword
Ground Beyond

Ken Jones

The positions set out in our chapters have been presented to various conferences of teachers and educationalists.[1] This conclusion is written shortly after the last of them – the History Workshop Conference on 'The Future of English', held in Oxford in June 1991. It seeks to engage with some powerful and strongly-held ideas that were voiced at the conference, ideas that are explicitly at odds with what we have spent the last four chapters advocating, and that represent, I should guess – the common sense of English teaching, post-'Cox'. It is a common sense which feels itself under renewed pressure from the right. John Major's speech to the Centre for Policy Studies, in which he attacked the 'mania for equality . . . a canker in our education system' signalled the end of a period in which educationalists could expect, almost unchallenged, to use their influence within the system to neutralise the demands of the right.[2] Major's combative tone was reinforced by actions: the chairman of the Centre for Policy Studies became the head of the Schools Examination and Assessment Council; 'controversial' Language in the National Curriculum (LINC) material on language teaching was withheld from schools by the DES; formal examinations, not coursework, would, Major announced, be the basis of GCSE.[3] These new restrictions on curriculum development were accompanied by wild attacks in the conservative press against prominent opponents: Terry Eagleton, NATE, and the Department of English and Media at the Institute of Education.[4]

It is in this context, always, since the mid-1980s defensive, but now especially beleaguered – that educationalists have developed their understandings of 'Cox'. For some, the Report embodies an unequivocal victory for progressive trends within English teaching, against the right. A second, more qualified, judgement admits – though usually without specification – the faults of 'Cox', but believes that it must be defended against Conservative attempts to undermine it. In this context, the LINC episode is an important battleground. A third argument recognises that there are weaknesses in the text of the Report, but insists that the attainment targets and programmes of study set out in the Parliamentary Order of March 1990 are worded with sufficient generality to allow the survival of even the more radical kinds of practice. From the point of view of their respective effects on the practice of schools, it is the Order, not the Report which preceded it, which is the important document.

In debates like these there is a great deal at stake: in teachers' still-developing responses to the National Curriculum, the educational climate of the next decade is being set. By way of conclusion, therefore, it is worth summarising our arguments in the form of an engagement with these more positive evaluations of 'Cox'. In some respects, we would not disagree with them: the Report does incorporate many elements of 'progressive' English teaching; its adoption will change for the better the way English is taught in many schools. The difficulty is to grasp that, what from one angle appears progress, from another looks like suppression. We know the more progressive implications of 'Cox'; we share the intention to defend them against Conservative critics. But we insist that we need to develop a more complex way of seeing the Report, a way that, to use an old term, attempts to be dialectical, and that in doing so recognises the 'suppressions' of 'Cox'. In an effort to render visible the contradictory effects of 'Cox', the way in which progress and regression can be combined in one and the same recommendation, the first chapter in this book made use of 'passive revolution'; it is a term that we wish to hold on to, as a means of grasping both the convolutions of the Report's text, and the way it has been received. Recognising the contradictions, our chapters concentrate not on the progress, but on what has been lost or left undeveloped. In this sense, they are necessary correctives to the relief or acclaim that has more usually greeted 'Cox'.

On the basis of positive, 'undialectical' understandings of 'Cox' arises a particular approach to the politics of English teaching, which centres on efforts to take advantage of the space the Report offers for the continuing development of 'progressive' approaches, and which defends it against the right. Only to the most rigorous purism can constructive engagement of this kind appear as some form of collaborationism; it is a necessary dimension of any response to 'Cox'. We want to suggest, though, that something has been lost in this process: a capacity to look not just at the space within 'Cox', but the ground beyond it. We have been told many times that 'Cox' has not ruled out anything, and that arguments like ours, by discussing the limits of the Report, have the unhelpful effect of suggesting that radical practice can find no home within its programme. One of the problems with a case like this is that it is happier with the exploration of marginal opportunities, than with thinking about a future for English outside the Report's framework. It substitutes the pragmatics of constructive engagement for the work of developing alternative practices. It tends to shirk a confrontation with positions set out in 'Cox' that are at odds with ways of thinking about class and culture developed by an important section of English teachers. It tends to be sanguine about the context of English; if the pressures of workload, assessment and new kinds of curriculum monitoring are noted, it is usually as problems that we can rise above, rather than debilitating burdens that need to be cast off.

The reader who has stayed with our book until now will have realised our disputes with this strategy, and our preference for continuing along routes it has declined to take. But our strategic choice is not self-validating. There is no point in going beyond 'Cox' if the positions that are thus arrived at are themselves intellectually, or politically, untenable. That, of course, is the accusation our critics make: the attention we pay to subordinate cultures involves abandoning concerns that centre on literary and educational value. To implement what we recommend would be to turn away from the cultural achievements of the European past, to promote cultural fragmentation and to entrench class or ethnic differences. By cutting students off from the achievements of the past, it would leave them trapped in the here-and-now of subordinate culture. At least, our critics might say, ' "Cox" envisages a common culture, and the sharing of meanings; you don't'.

This is an argument we have considered, and argued with, since beginning to write the book, but it is not one that we have come to accept. To begin with, in criticising 'Cox', we do not think we are suggesting the replacement of its version of a common culture by an endorsement of cultural fragmentation. A radical, fragmentary pluralism may, as Alan Sinfield puts it, 'exercise a leverage upon the dominant, denying it a monopoly of credibility[5] but the very nature of its project prevents it going further; it does not aim at counter-hegemony. By contrast, a project of general, organised, collectively-based social transformation involves elaborating a set of understandings and meanings that cross the frontiers between at least some of the different cultures in a 'multi-cultural' society. It is within such a project that we would locate the chapters of this book: they are not celebrations of the 'politics of identity', but rather explorations of classroom encounters *between* identities. 'Cox' seeks to manage difference – recognising it only to incorporate it into a pre-established, unquestioned whole. We prefer to address difference more explicitly. As Chris Richards suggests, the 'disjunction between informal culture and the school curriculum' should form less the uneasy, half-noted backdrop to the English curriculum, than one of its central elements. In this context, 'value' is not a term to be avoided. On the contrary, it suggests a focus of continual discussion, in which different orientations towards knowledge and culture engage. Our guess is that classrooms of this type would be places where critical attitudes towards the dominant culture were generated, and where elements of an alternative, shared system of meanings might emerge. They would, we think, provide better opportunities for the creative and cognitive development of school-students than those that are offered by 'Cox'.

It is this last point which we think offers the basis for a *politically*, as well as an intellectually, tenable alternative to 'Cox' and to the National Curriculum in general. The promise of the National Curriculum is its ability to provide a better education for everyone. A high level of curricular uniformity is held to be essential to this purpose, and the example of centralised European systems is quoted to prove the link between uniformity of provision, and higher standards for all. It is worth recalling the other side of this European tradition. In France, as Balibar and Laporte have made clear, universality and rationality were the masks worn by an education that was systematic in its neglect and denial of the experience of subordinate classes and regional populations.[6] The curriculum of such a system was and is highly selective in its attitude to the cultures, interests and social objectives of these groups; the protesting students of 1990 were only the latest to make this point.[7] Looked at from this perspective, the inadequacies of a highly specified National Curriculum are clear. Claiming its relevance to all students, it in fact neglects the specific conditions of their lives and the interests which motivate their learning. It presents to students a model of knowledge which, in its particular orientation towards their lives, is unlikely to be attractive. Thus its claim to deliver a better education is, and will continue to be, contested at the level of the classroom. It is in the context of such a contestation that the alternatives to Cox that we have been discussing make sense. They would not base themselves on a 'universalism' that concealed the presence of specific social interests, nor would limit themselves to a 'curriculum of everyday life', confined to the local and particular. They would move among and between cultures, bringing them into a process of encounter and confrontation, and aiming to explore in that process the connections between general social relationships and the lives of school-students. In an educational arena in which the noise about 'standards' has so far overwhelmed considerations of the relationship between cultural conflict and educational experience, this is a goal worth arguing for. It might even inform a new politics of education.

Notes

1. In addition to the Chicago and Oxford conferences, aspects of our chapters have been discussed at the BERA symposium on 'Social Justice and the School', Roehampton, 1990 and at the London Association for the teaching of English conference on 'Unequal Opportunities?', London, 1991.
2. John Major, Speech to the Centre for Policy Studies on *Education – All Our Futures*, 3 July 1991.
3. For the appointment of 'Lord Griffiths of Fforestfach' as chair of SEAC, see *TES* 26 July 1991; on the suppression of LINC material, see *TES* 14 June 1991; on the limitation of GCSE coursework to 20 per cent, see Major's speech.
4. See, for example, John Clare's report on the Ruskin Conference in the *Daily Telegraph*, 20 June 1991, John Marks' apparently second-hand version in the *TES* 5 July 1991, and Nicholas Farrell's claim that 'progressives are subverting education', with Eagleton at the head of them, in 'The Scargill of the 1990s?', *Sunday Telegraph*, 30 June 1991. *The Guardian* contributed its own shameful profile of Eagleton on 15 August 1991.
5. A. Sinfield, *Literature, Politics and Culture in Postwar Britain*, 1989, pp. 302–3.
6. R. Balibar and D. Laporte *Le Francais National (Politique et Pratiques de la langue nationale sous la revolution Francaise)*, 1974.
7. *Lycees turn backs on the working class*, *TES* 14 December 1990.

Index